Venus

Earth

Asteroid Belt

Saturn

Neptune

Observing the
Universe

Observing the
Universe

Ray Spangenburg and Kit Moser

Franklin Watts

A DIVISION OF SCHOLASTIC INC.
NEW YORK · TORONTO · LONDON · AUCKLAND
SYDNEY · MEXICO CITY · NEW DELHI · HONG KONG
DANBURY, CONNECTICUT

To amateur astronomers everywhere

Photographs © 2003: AP/Wide World Photos/Chris Dorst: 45, 109; Art Resource, NY/ Werner Forman: 18 top; Bridgeman Art Library International Ltd., London/New York: 18 bottom (Ashmolean Museum, Oxford, UK), 16 (Bibliotheque Municipale, Boulogne sur Mer, France), 19 (British Museum, London, UK); Corbis Images: 35, 73, 119 (AFP), 83 (AFP/NASA), 23 (Archivo Iconografico, S.A.), 20, 21, top 105 (Bettmann), 39 (Dennis di Cicco), 27 (Hulton-Deutsch Collection), 29, 30, 54 (Roger Ressmeyer); NASA: 74 (W.P. Blair), 75 (J.P. Harrington & K.J. Borkowski), 13, 102 (Hubble Heritage Team), 70, 71 (IPAC), 68 (Robert Williams and the Hubble Deep Field Team); Photo Researchers, NY: 21 bottom (Dr. Jeremy Burgess/SPL), 53, 115 (Simon Fraser), 91 (Gerard Lodriguss), 78, 86, 123 (NASA), 33 (Max Planck Institute); Photri Inc.: 2 (Scott Berner), cover (Hubble Space Station), 80, 124 (John Hughes/NASA), 10, 14, 28, 48, 49, 56, 63, 89, 110, 116 (NASA), 50 (Nik Szymanek).

The photograph on the cover shows an image taken by the Hubble Space Telescope of the brightest star yet known. The photograph opposite the title page shows the Gamma Ray Observatory satellite.

Library of Congress Cataloging-in-Publication Data
    Spangenburg, Ray, 1939–
    Observing the universe / Ray Spangenburg and Kit Moser.
    p. cm. — (Out of this world)
Summary: A comprehensive look at the exploration of the universe, from observations of ancient skywatchers to the first orbiting observatories and voyages of robot spacecraft to the outer solar system.
Includes bibliographical references and index.
    ISBN 0-531-11927-0 (lib. bdg.)   0-531-16687-2 (pbk.)
    1. Outer space—Juvenile literature. [1. Outer space.]
I. Moser, Diane, 1944– II. Title. III. Out of this world (Franklin Watts, Inc.)
QB500.22.S67   2003   523.1—dc21
2003005810

Acknowledgments

To all those who have contributed to *Observing the Universe,* we would like to take this opportunity to say "thank you," with special appreciation to our editors on this project, Melissa Palestro and Christine Florie for their enthusiasm and fine work. We would also like to give credit to Melissa Stewart, whose originality and vision provided the initial sparks for this series. Additionally, we would like to thank Margaret Carruthers, planetary geologist, Washington, DC, and Dr. Richard Ash of the University of Maryland, who reviewed the manuscript and provided many insightful suggestions. If any inaccuracies remain, the fault is ours, not theirs. Also, to Tony Reichhardt and John Rhea, once our editors at the former *Space World Magazine,* thanks for starting us out on many fascinating journeys into space, space science, and technology—including both a visit to see the Hubble Space Telescope when it was still in a Lockheed clean room on the West Coast and a flight on a research mission aboard the *Kuiper Airborne Observatory.*

Contents

Observing the
Universe

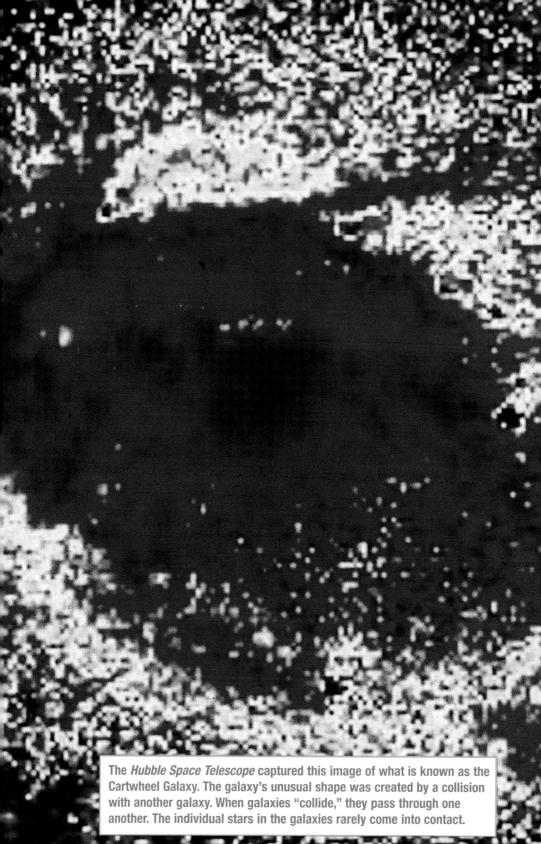

The *Hubble Space Telescope* captured this image of what is known as the Cartwheel Galaxy. The galaxy's unusual shape was created by a collision with another galaxy. When galaxies "collide," they pass through one another. The individual stars in the galaxies rarely come into contact.

Faraway Worlds
and Galactic
Empires

G o out some clear night and take a look up at the sky. There you can see some of the same lights that people have seen and wondered about through the ages. You may see just a couple of stars or planets. In the city, lights from businesses, homes, and cars and trucks flood the skies with a competing blaze. However, even there, you can see a few stars on a clear night. If you have a chance to look at the stars on a clear night in the mountains, away from city lights, you see a starry splendor arching overhead. This is what ancient skywatchers saw above them night after night. No electric or sodium lights competed, and they had a stunning view.

Today, astronomers have many ways to watch the stars. They have placed giant observatories on high mountaintops, away from city lights and above some of the vapor and movement of Earth's atmosphere. They have devised ways to magnify what they see and record it electronically. They have learned new ways to look at the skies, so they can see events and objects in the universe that no one could see with their eyes—even through a telescope. With these exciting techniques they have captured stunning—and revealing—vistas.

Scientists have also sent spacecraft to orbit Earth and turn their powerful instruments toward all parts of the universe—almost completely unblocked by Earth's atmosphere or light pollution.

Through images taken both by mountaintop observatories and spaceborne telescopes, millions of people have now seen the huge, horse-shaped cloud of stars and dust called the Horsehead Nebula. They have seen enormous stalks of gas and dust where stars are "born" in the Eagle Nebula. Small, starlike objects called brown dwarfs show up now in space telescope images—"almost-stars" that never got big enough to become true stars. In ages past, they used to be too small for anyone to see even with a powerful mountaintop telescope.

These eyes never blink. These many eyes see in ways our own eyes could never see. They "see" radio waves and X rays. They capture infrared, ultraviolet, and gamma-ray radiation. They capture endless exciting events that took place millions of light-years away. Look, there a supernova explodes with unimaginable power. Galaxies collide in an enormous blast. *Quasars* are blinking, blinking, and scientists can see evidence that matter is indeed falling into massive black holes. Pulsars are whirling like lighthouse beacons, far far away.

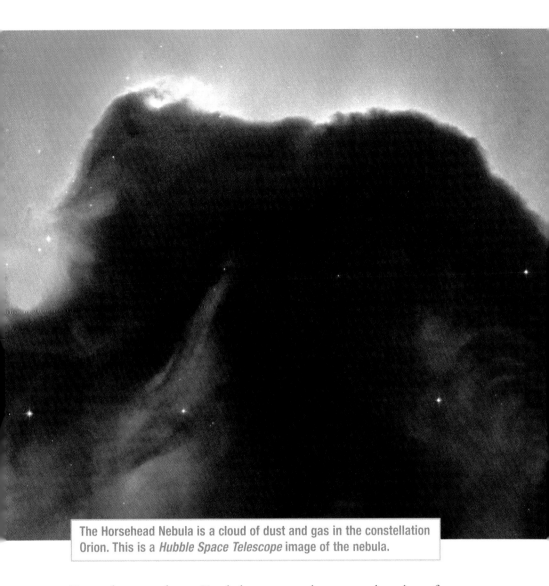

The Horsehead Nebula is a cloud of dust and gas in the constellation Orion. This is a *Hubble Space Telescope* image of the nebula.

Every day, people on Earth buzz around on our planet's surface. They run to catch a bus, lunch tucked under their arms, waving to a friend on the way. They hurry to work or school. They tell jokes with friends, watch movies, ride bikes, run laps, and kick soccer balls. Traf-

These unusual shapes are actually pillarlike clouds of gas in the Eagle Nebula. Within, new stars are being formed.

fic hums on the freeways and on downtown streets. Streetcars clang and subways whoosh. It is easy to forget that ours is a very small planet swirling around an average star, one of billions of stars in the universe. It is easy to forget that beyond Earth's surface and Earth's atmosphere, a vast universe of stars and galaxies stretches beyond the limits of our most powerful astronomical instruments. Their piercing light travels through nearly unimaginable distances to our tiny region of the universe. Through delicate instruments, scientists have learned how to view these objects in dozens of different ways—each view providing new ways of understanding the universe, how it may have begun, and what it is made of. Each new view provides new clues and new insights—and, always, opens up hundreds of new questions. Each new observation unlocks untold visual beauty, not imagined even by the most insightful forecasters.

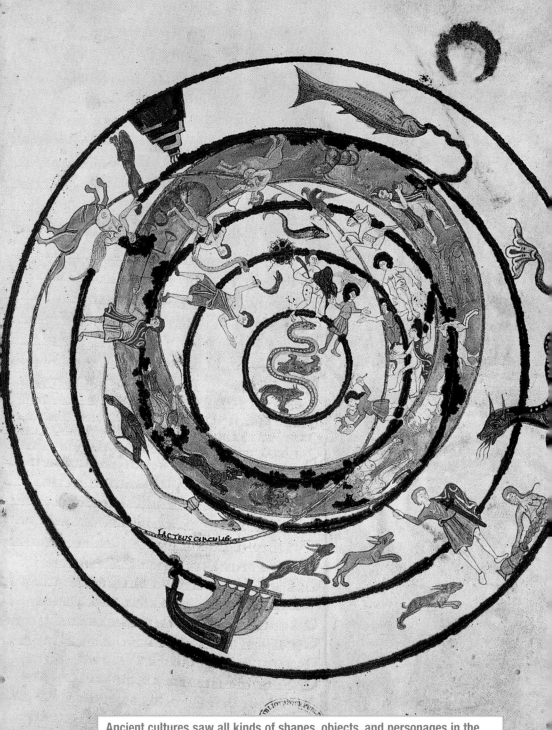

Ancient cultures saw all kinds of shapes, objects, and personages in the stars visible in the night sky, and they created a vast body of folklore, myth, and religious belief about them. This is an illustration of the constellations from a tenth-century French manuscript of the work of fourth-century Greek scientist Eudoxus, who was the first to create a map of the stars.

Chapter 1

Skywatching and Wonder

From before the beginning of human history, people have looked up at the nighttime skies. They began thinking and wondering about the tiny specks of light they saw. What were these pinpricks of light? What did they mean? People of all cultures came up with ideas about what they could be—and they were all different, wonderful mixtures of common sense, imagination, and observation.

Perhaps the sky was covered by a huge, dark blanket, draped on poles that were out of sight, pricked by holes that let the daytime light shine through. Maybe the night sky was a huge upside-down bowl. Perhaps the heavens were composed of perfect globes, or spheres, of crystal, nested one inside the other, with stars hanging far out, on the outermost sphere. Each culture came up with its own explanation.

In the Aztec culture of ancient Mexico, the god Quetzalcoatl was sometimes depicted as a serpent bursting forth from the Sun.

Some early cultures made careful studies of the movements of the stars, Sun, Moon, and planets. They watched, compared, and recorded them. As long as 4,000 years ago, Babylonian astronomers in the Middle East gathered facts they observed about the stars. They carved their records on clay tablets, and these records of changing star positions became a way of studying cycles and the passage of time. Then they created calendars based on their records. Using these, they could understand Earth's cycles and predict when the rivers would flood across the croplands and when crops should be planted and harvested.

Early astronomers also soon began to develop tools for measuring distances between stars and

The ancient Babylonians recorded the rising and the falling of the planet Venus in the sky on stone tablets such as this one.

To explain the apparent movement of the Sun across the sky from east to west in the course of the day, the ancient Egyptians depicted it as a god carried by servants across the sky on a boat.

other objects and for calculating their movements. However, not until the invention of the telescope could anyone really see much of what was happening in the vast universe around us. Stars appeared to be faint pinpoints of light shining through a dark canopy. The planets seemed to be "wandering stars" because they looked a lot like stars— yet their orbits made them seem to wander around in the sky, against the steadier background of stars. No one had ever seen the surface of a planet other than Earth or a close-up photo of the Moon's surface. People did not understand that those specks of light were other worlds. The invention of the *telescope* in the seventeenth century began to change all that. Only then did astronomers begin to see that these objects were all worlds in their own right.

Birth of a Great Astronomical Tool: The Telescope

Telescopes have only been around for about 400 years. The word "telescope" comes originally from a Greek word, *teleskopos,* from *tele* (a word meaning "farseeing") and *skopos* (meaning "watcher"). Some records suggest that the idea behind the telescope—using glass lenses in a tube to see faraway objects—may first have occurred to early spectacle makers in Italy. Roger Bacon (c. 1220–1292)—an English philosopher known for his promotion of experimental science—may

also have played with the concept in the thirteenth century. According to traditions gathered from seventeenth-century stories, though, the creation of the first telescope was a happy accident. In about 1608, a Dutch eyeglass maker named Hans Lippershey (c. 1570–c.1619) happened to line up two lenses having just the right qualities. When he looked through it, or so the story goes, he real-

The thirteenth-century English philosopher Roger Bacon was one of the first advocates of observation and experimentation as the basic building blocks of science.

ized he had invented an instrument that made faraway objects seem much closer.

Soon people began using telescopes for spotting faraway ships as they appeared along the horizon, carrying traveling loved ones and goods for trade. Within a few months, the great Italian astronomer Galileo Galilei (1564–1642) heard about Lippershey's trick with lenses. He began building his own optic tubes, patterned after Lippershey's original.

Galileo's telescope was just a long tube fitted with two lenses. With this tool, he found that the objects he looked at appeared up to 3 times larger than before. Then, Galileo had a brilliant idea. Why not use his telescope to look at planets and stars? Beginning in 1609, he began to spend his nights peering through his telescope at the wonders of the nighttime skies.

By today's standards, Galileo's telescope was crude. A telescope you can buy in a toy

The Italian Renaissance genius Galileo Galilei was an astronomer, mathematician, and physicist.

store has better lenses with fewer flaws. But at the time, it was a completely revolutionary instrument for astronomy and for everyday life. Today, the telescope is still the most important tool an astronomer has. Through the telescope, Galileo could see faint objects not even visible before. It also showed him nearby objects much larger and more clearly than anyone had ever before seen them. Using his new "eyes," he made many discoveries. Galileo realized that no one else had ever seen the details he could see through his telescope. He looked carefully at each object and made many detailed drawings.

He saw that the Moon did not have a smooth surface, as everyone had always thought it did. He could see the pitted surface scarred by many craters. He also saw high, craggy mountains, hills, broad valleys, and vast smooth areas.

Galileo was the first to notice that Venus, like the Moon, has phases. That is, Venus sometimes appears as just a thin sliver of light. Sometimes we see a half circle of light. And sometimes we see the entire disk—a flat-looking circle. These phases, we now know, are caused by the movements of Earth and Venus as each moves in its orbit around the Sun. The changing shapes we see are combinations of reflected sunlight and shadow across the surface of Venus as it changes positions with respect to both Earth (from which we observers are watching) and the Sun.

During his nighttime observations, Galileo discovered the four largest moons of Jupiter—Io, Europa, Ganymede, and Callisto. These big moons are known as the "Galilean" moons in his honor. No one had ever realized before that other planets also had moons. Galileo also noticed a strange bump on each side of Saturn's disk. He was puzzled,

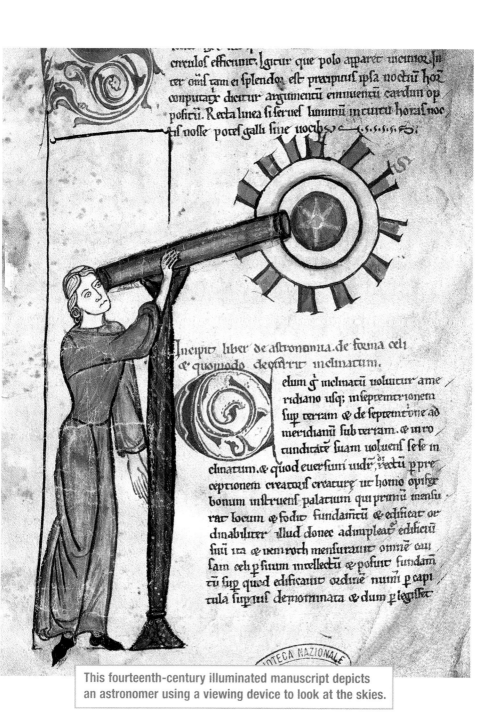

This fourteenth-century illuminated manuscript depicts an astronomer using a viewing device to look at the skies.

A telescope that uses glass lenses to produce an image, as Galileo's did, is called a refracting telescope, or refractor. In a refractor, light rays from an object pass through a large main lens, called the primary objective, the first lens or lens system to receive light from the object being viewed. In a refracting telescope, the primary objective may also be called the primary lens. This lens is *convex* (thicker at the middle than at the edges). The shape of the lens bends, or "refracts," the light so that it comes together at a focal point, behind which a small, upside-down image of the object appears. The eyepiece at the end of the tube, consisting of one or more smaller lenses, magnifies this image so the observer can see it more easily.

In a reflecting telescope, or *reflector,* the objective is not a lens. Instead it is a large mirror, called the primary mirror. The shape is curved, or *concave,* scooped out like a bowl. Light from an object reflects off this mirror, and then it may be reflected off a secondary mirror. From there, the light bounces back to the eyepiece. The secondary mirror may be flat, convex, or concave. The shape depends on the way the telescope designer wants the light to travel through the reflecting telescope. Finally, the image is magnified by the lenses of the eyepiece. The *Hubble Space Telescope*, for example, is a reflector. In either a refractor or a reflector, a camera may take the place of the eyepiece.

Reflectors may also use an additional small, flat mirror to bend the light. This allows the viewer to see the image from an eyepiece at the side of the telescope, a design still used by many small reflecting telescopes. They are known as "Newtonian" telescopes in honor of Isaac Newton, who first came up with this design.

Very large observatory telescopes may have special mechanisms for allowing observers to see through the eyepiece. Sometimes astronomers use an elevator to reach a special cage or platform high up on the telescope just below the observatory dome and near the primary objective. The observer may sit in the cage at the primary focus of the telescope.

Refracting telescopes are usually best for viewing solar system objects, and reflecting telescopes are more often used for deep space astronomy. By the last half of the twentieth century, several very large reflecting telescopes had been built on mountaintop observatories where the air is especially clear. Some primary lenses or mirrors have diameters of more than 200 inches (5 m) or more. In Galileo's and Newton's time, though, such large dimensions were not yet possible—and these great scientists had no hint of the methods for "seeing" the universe in ways that did not involve optical instruments and visible light. These were adventures that were yet to come!

but scientists later learned that these bumps were actually Saturn's "rings," an enormous system of space rocks, pebbles, and dust that orbit the giant planet.

He was the first to realize that the cloudy light of the Milky Way was actually a vast crowd of stars—a conclusion he came to because he could see the distinct points of light that no one had ever seen before. He studied sunspots on the Sun—dark, stormy areas that appear from time to time in the outer gassy regions of the Sun—and he mapped their movements. (*Warning:* Never look directly at the Sun. You can cause serious damage to your eyes—even blindness.)

Over the years following Galileo's observations, telescopes began to improve. They became bigger, could gather more light, and astronomers could see even more clearly. Lens makers soon found that simple glass lenses tended to distort the image. They didn't have precision tools. Each lens had to be ground by hand, and precision was practically impossible, so they had difficulty grinding perfectly smooth curves. Also, big pieces of glass are so heavy they tend to sag. They don't sag a lot—but enough to distort an image. Some astronomers grew concerned over the challenges of making perfect lenses.

One solution to this problem was to use something else. A Scottish mathematician named James Gregory (1638–1675) invented a different type of telescope in 1663. He knew that a large, smooth mirror is a lot easier to make than a perfect lens. He also knew that just one side of a mirror has to give a clear view—the reflecting side. Builders could place a framework behind the mirror to support the sagging glass. They couldn't use this kind of support on a lens because the light has to shine *through* a lens.

A few years later, in 1668, English physicist and astronomer Isaac Newton (1642–1727) made the first successful *reflector,* or reflecting, telescope—using mirrors.

From then on, telescopes got bigger and bigger—and therefore could gather more and more light. The more light a telescope could gather, the more the observer could see. You can think of a telescope as a big "light bucket." The lenses and mirrors gather the light and pass it on to the eyepiece. Artisans became more skilled at fashioning and polishing the mirrors and lenses they used. The more perfectly smoothed and polished the *optics* (the lenses and mirrors), the more accurate the images became that were passed on to the observer.

In 1757, an amateur astronomer named William Herschel (1738–1822) fled from war in his native Germany to England. He was a professional musician who played the oboe, organ, and violin and was also a conductor and composer. By 1766 he had built his reputation as a musician in England and was hired as organist at a chapel in the city of Bath in southwest England. His sister, Caroline Herschel (1750–1848), joined him there in 1772. William, in the meantime, had eagerly read hundreds of books on his favorite pastime, astronomy. He also had taught himself about optics and calculus. Both Herschels became caught up in William's enthusiasm and built their first telescope together shortly after Caroline arrived. The next one they built was larger, and the next even larger. Their largest reflecting telescope had a mirror 48 inches (1.2 m) in diameter and a tube 40 feet (12 m) long. Herschel's telescopes had especially large diameters. When asked about the unusual structure of his telescopes, Herschel would explain that he was not after magnification alone. He wanted light-gathering capability. The larger the telescope's mirror, the more light it was capa-

This is the giant telescope built by the British astronomer William Herschel. The most famous astronomer of the eighteenth century, Herschel discovered the planet Uranus and was the first person to correctly describe the shape of the Milky Way.

ble of capturing from faint objects in the sky. The more light the telescope captured, the better he could see the stars and *nebulae* (Latin for "mist," because they looked like misty clouds) against the dark skies.

Creating and polishing a mirror that size was quite a job, and Herschel had no special equipment for the task. He and Caroline set to

Lord Rosse, a nineteenth-century English nobleman, built the largest telescopes of his time at his observatory at Birr Castle in Ireland. This is the 72-inch (1.8 m) telescope Rosse completed in 1845. It weighed 72 tons.

work in the basement of the Herschel home. They poured a molten mixture of tin and other metals into a mold made from horse manure—at least, according to legend. Then they ground the hardened metal into a parabola. Finally, they made it bright and shiny by polishing it for weeks—a job they had to repeat every few days because the tin mixture quickly blackened with tarnish. The telescope was so

The 100-inch (2.5 m) Hooker telescope at Mount Wilson Observatory in California was completed in 1917. Some of Edwin Hubble's most important work was based on observations made using the Hooker.

large, Herschel had to build a scaffold to hold it and climb a ladder to observe the skies. Night after night, he would sweep the skies with his telescope in carefully planned strips. He was organized and disciplined. Each night he would pick up where he had left off the night before. The effort paid off, though. Looking through one of his own telescopes in 1781, Herschel discovered the planet Uranus. It was the first planet ever observed that ancient sky-watchers had not already seen and named. Later, Herschel discovered two of Uranus's moons, as well as two moons of Saturn. Using his immense telescopes, this gifted and tireless astronomer also discovered many clusters and galaxies of stars, and some 2,400 nebulae.

Herschel's big telescopes allowed him to probe deeper into space. "I have looked farther into space than ever [a] human being did before me," he once wrote. Herschel's first love was the pursuit

This is the famous Hale telescope at Palomar Observatory in California.

of the starry realm. And the big telescopes allowed him to peer into its depths.

Herschel's telescope would not remain the biggest, though. Another master builder, Lord Rosse (William Parsons, 3rd Earl of Rosse, 1800–1867) in Ireland, built an even bigger telescope in 1844. It was known as the Leviathan of Birr Castle. Its enormous 72-inch (1.8-m) mirror held the record for nearly a century. The Leviathan remained the world's largest telescope until 1917, when the 100-inch (2.5-m) Hooker telescope was built at Mount Wilson Observatory northwest of Los Angeles, California. Then the Hale telescope at neighboring Palomar Observatory set a new record 31 years later. The Hale, completed in 1948, measured 200 inches (5 m) across. At the time, it was by far the largest telescope in the world.

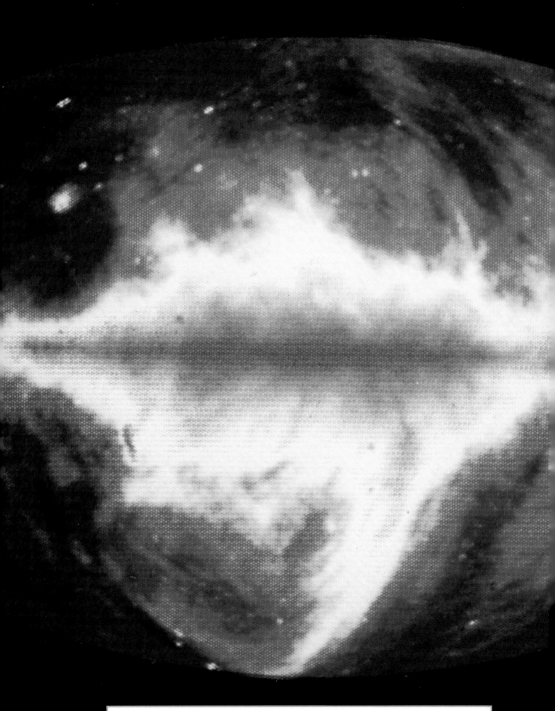

This is an all-sky radio map. Radio waves, X rays, gamma rays, ultraviolet rays, and visible light are all forms of electromagnetic radiation.

Chapter 2

Ways of "Seeing"

For thousands of years, the only objects in the universe that astronomers knew about were those that could be seen with the eyes. Then, with the magnification of the telescope, scientists began to discover some things that they couldn't see with the naked eye. Yet they were still looking at only a portion of what exists.

Not until the 1930s did astronomers begin to realize that they had been only examining a small portion of the objects that exist in the universe and had seen those they had studied in a very limited way— as if they had been listening to a symphony orchestra but had heard only the violins.

Using the Whole Electromagnetic Spectrum

The light we see is just a small part of an important family of energies known as the *electromagnetic spectrum* (the full range of the waves and frequencies of electromagnetic radiation). Visible light is just about in the middle of the spectrum—the portion of the spectrum that we describe as the different colors of the rainbow, from red to violet. White light (sunlight and starlight) is a mixture of many of these colors. The rest of the electromagnetic spectrum is made up of types of radiation that humans cannot see. Yet you will find many of the names familiar.

Infrared rays, microwave radiation, and radio waves occur at one end of the spectrum. Their wavelengths are longer than red light waves, which have the longest visible wavelengths. At the other end of the spectrum are types of radiation with such short wavelengths that they are also invisible to humans, including ultraviolet (UV) waves, X rays, and gamma rays.

Some of these types of radiation cannot penetrate Earth's atmosphere. So telescopes on Earth's surface are not well suited to "view" wavelengths emitted by objects in space. Not until the space age arrived, with rockets to send satellites into orbit, did astronomers have a good chance to explore what else besides radio waves the objects in space might give off.

Some observatories on the high mountaintops of the world began to add instruments that recorded emissions from other regions of the spectrum besides visible light and radio waves. Yet the best opportunities came when space telescopes began to orbit Earth. From its position above the atmosphere, a space telescope can get a clear view. It can use specialized instruments to measure radiation levels in different regions of the spectrum, without interference from Earth's atmosphere. Very cool objects give off infrared waves, even though they may emit very little radiation of other types. So images of infrared radiation can reveal very cool objects that might otherwise be barely detected using conventional, visible light astronomy. UV energies are given off by very hot and exotic types of sky objects, such as white dwarf stars, planetary nebulas, and explosive phenomena.

In 1967, one of the early U.S. space observatories, the third Orbiting Solar Observatory (OSO-3), discovered the first firm evidence of gamma rays in space. Since that time, gamma-ray astronomy has mushroomed in importance. Today, it provides yet another clear window for observing the universe. Gamma rays are the most energetic of all the forms of radiation in the electromagnetic spectrum, and they are produced by highly energetic processes. Nuclear fusion and nuclear fission both produce gamma rays. So does radioactive decay. Collisions of high-energy particles also produce gamma rays. Observation of gamma rays offers an especially good way for observing far distant

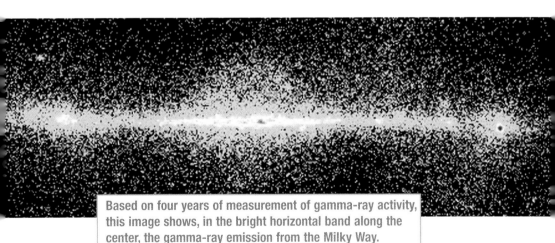

Based on four years of measurement of gamma-ray activity, this image shows, in the bright horizontal band along the center, the gamma-ray emission from the Milky Way.

objects. Gamma-ray astronomy also provides a means of peering into some of the most violent and destructive processes in the universe. It displays material as it falls into black holes, and it reveals the creation of elements and their destruction within stars and galaxies.

Visible light also plays important roles beyond "what you see is what you get." Since astronomers can't put their subjects in laboratories and test them, they have to learn as much as they can from the light they give off, or the light they absorb. They use many artful techniques to squeeze as much information as they can out of the spectrum measured from a cosmic object. Using an instrument called a spectrometer, or spectrograph, they examine the light from an object. A spectrograph is an instrument that separates light into its various colors and photographs or maps the spectrum so astronomers can analyze it. Although the Sun looks yellow to us, its light actually contains many colors. Other stars may emit light containing different colors. By breaking the light down into the separate colors that are actually present, this highly useful instrument can reveal just how hot a star is, how fast and in what direction it is moving, and what elements it is made up of.

This is done by passing sunlight, for example, through a prism to break it up into its components, then passing the differentiated light directly through a diffraction grating to produce a readable spectrum, and photographing or mapping the results. The resulting photograph or map shows separate vertical lines of different colors captured after passing through the slits of the grating. Black areas of the reading indicate that the color in that part of the spectrum was absorbed before leaving the Sun and was not emitted in the sunlight. Each object's spectrum contains features that are characteristic of particular atoms, ions, and molecules. So by identifying and measuring each individual line, an astronomer can tell what a star, planet, nebula, or galaxy is made of—by the light it gives off or reflects.

Using all these techniques discovered in the past 70 years, astronomers find themselves able to look at objects in the universe in a much fuller way than ever before. Astronomers can examine the same object using instruments that can see UV radiation, gamma-ray radiation, X-ray radiation, radio waves, infrared waves, microwaves, or visible light. They can measure the visible-light spectrum. From overlapping views, they are finding that a much more complete picture emerges—a picture that shows energetic processes, temperature, composition, and many other revealing factors. From this information, they are constantly discovering new answers to some of the biggest questions about the universe—and some of the most intriguing mysteries.

Discovering the Electromagnetic Spectrum

Actually, by the early 1800s scientists had already found evidence that much more was going on here on Earth than humans could see. William Herschel had discovered infrared light in 1800, a slightly longer electromagnetic wave than the human eye can see. A year later, in 1801, German chemist Johann Ritter (1776–1810) discovered the existence of ultraviolet (UV) light. UV light, Ritter found, has a short wavelength and is also invisible to humans. About a century later, in 1895, German physicist Wilhelm Conrad Roentgen (1845–1923) discovered the existence of X rays. Three years later, French chemists Marie and Pierre Curie did pioneering work on radioactivity and discovered the element radium, one of the sources of gamma rays. Yet, astronomers had not detected these types of radiation in the cosmos. The first breakthrough came from radio waves, first discovered and used in 1888 by physicist Heinrich Hertz (1857–1894).

Radio Waves from the Skies

In 1931 Karl Jansky (1905–1950), an engineer at Bell Telephone Laboratories in New Jersey, was working on ways to reduce static in radio transmissions. Static interfered with radio transmissions and made them hard to hear and understand. That was a big problem for ship-to-shore and transatlantic radio telephones (which is why Bell Labs got involved). Jansky set up an antenna with a very sensitive receiver and a recorder. With it, he was able to trace the sources of static, and he found three: local storms, distant thunderstorms, and one other. The third source was a mystery at first. It was very faint, just a faint hissing. Jansky noticed that it moved consistently, a little each day. In fact it appeared four minutes earlier each day—at the same rate that the canopy of stars moves beyond the solar system. Jansky began to realize that he was detecting a radio source from beyond Earth's surface, even beyond the edge of the solar system. Then he noticed that he heard this faint hissing whenever the antenna pointed in the direction of the constellation Sagittarius—approximately at the center of our own galaxy, the Milky Way.

It was a stunning discovery. Jansky had found that some cosmic objects actually give off radio waves. Up to that point, astronomers had assumed that "what you see is what you get." They didn't realize that some objects do not give off visible light, but do give off other kinds of radiation. In this case, they gave off radio waves—which are also

This is the Milky Way Galaxy as seen from the ground in Springfield, Vermont. The Milky Way is the galaxy in which our solar system lies.

part of the electromagnetic spectrum. Jansky's news was published in 1933—it even made the front page of *The New York Times* on May 5, 1933. However, the discovery stirred up very little attention in the scientific community. Astronomers were caught up in optical observations and knew very little about radio techniques, so for years they completely missed the significance of Jansky's discoveries, and Jansky moved on to other projects.

However, one young radio engineer and amateur radio operator from Wheaton, Illinois, did take notice. By 1937, Grote Reber (1911–2002) had built his own radio telescope. It was steerable—that is, he could point it at different parts of the sky. Instead of optics for seeing, it had a bowl-shaped dish for listening. Reber began sweeping the skies for cosmic sources of radio signals. Of course, he wasn't really listening literally. The radio waves were collected by the antenna and signals were graphed by an instrument on paper. He used his antenna to map the regions of the sky from which they came. Reber worked alone, the sole radio astronomer in existence during the years before World War II.

During the war, radar (which stands for *ra*dio *d*etecting *a*nd *r*anging) came into use for detecting the distance and location of aircraft. Radar is an electronic system that measures distance by bouncing radio waves off objects and timing how long the signal takes to make a round-trip. After the war, uses of radio were much better understood, and radio astronomy began to grow. In fact, early studies of the planets were made by using radar techniques. In 1946 in Australia, a physicist named E. G. Bowen began doing some radio astronomy studies of the Sun. Then in 1947, radio astronomers homed in on the first radio object that could also be observed by eye: the Crab Nebula. Today, radio maps of the sky can be used to create images that help us "see" ranges of temperatures and heat divisions in far-off galaxies and stars.

The universe is a big place. In fact, it is all there is—everything that exists, including Earth, planets, stars, galaxies, everything they contain, and everything in between, including gases and dust. Let's take a quick tour of what's out there in space that astronomers—amateurs like you or me and professionals—are so eager to examine and know more about.

You Are Here: Planet Earth

The ground we stand on is part of planet Earth. If we were on the Moon looking at Earth, we would see swirls of white clouds, splashes of blue that we know are oceans, and large brownish areas—land. American astronomer Carl Sagan (1934–1996) once called this planet a "pale blue dot." It seems big and all-encompassing and powerful because it is our home and we see it up close. But actually, it is a fragile ecosystem, a balance of living and nonliving things—the only planet like it that we know of so far.

Our Close Neighbors: The Planets

In the vast expanse known as the universe, our closest neighbors are the other members of the solar system—the system, or family, of *planets, moons, asteroids, meteoroids,* and *comets* that revolve around the Sun (called Sol by the Romans, so that's where the word "solar" comes from). If you could hover over the Sun and look out over the solar family, the closest object would be Mercury, a tiny, rocky planet close to the Sun. Next is Venus, always hidden under a deep layer of clouds, Earth's closest neighbor. Then Earth and its Moon. A bit farther out is the red planet, Mars, and its two small moons. A wide belt of smaller, rocky objects orbits the Sun between Mars and the next planet. Most of these "space rocks," called asteroids, are dark and oddly shaped. This region is known as the asteroid belt. Beyond these rocks is the outer solar system, a region of large, gassy planets often called "gas giants," which all have at least faint rings and many moons. The first and largest is Jupiter, the "king of planets," followed by the planet Saturn and its wide bands of spectacular rings. Beyond Saturn, we would see two more gas giants, Uranus and Neptune, both cold and blue. At the edge of the visible solar system two faint objects appear, the tiny rocky planet Pluto and its small moon. Beyond these lies a mysterious region known as the Kuiper Belt, encircling the entire system with mysterious objects too distant, small, and dark to make out with the instruments astronomers currently have. Then, in a distant belt known as the Oort Cloud, scientists estimate that millions of inactive comets dwell in a sort of perpetual "deep freeze"—until one day something disturbs one or two, changing their orbits, and they come slinging in toward the Sun, pay a brief visit, and then travel outward again. Over the centuries, astronomers have found many ways of looking at this nearby family, and we have found out a lot about them—but there is always much more to learn.

The Sun, at the center of the solar system, is the closest *star* to us and, since it is in our own backyard, observers have been able to learn a lot about stars by learning about the Sun. The many solar observation satellites, spacecraft missions, and space shuttle experiments that have been focused on the Sun in the last 45 years alone have provided a wealth of images and information about our star and about stars in general—especially medium-sized stars like the Sun.

Galaxies

The wonders to be discovered do not stop at the edge of the solar system. We are on a planet, amid other planets, moons, and "space rocks" orbiting around a star— and that system and star are located in a large cluster of stars, dust, and gas known as a galaxy, or, rather, the *Galaxy*. (Because the Milky Way is so central to us, astronomers capitalize the word "galaxy" when it refers to our own.) We call it the Milky Way because it appears in Earth's nighttime skies as a brightly glowing band of white, as if the gods had spilled a bucket of milk across the heavens. However, that is only a concentration of stars seen from our particular angle, through the plane of the disk—where the stars are most concentrated. Actually, every star we can see in the sky is located within our Galaxy. The Galaxy formed about 14 billion years ago, and it is about 100,000 light years in diameter—that is, a photon (a particle of light) takes 100,000 years to travel from one side of the Galaxy to the other. It is a spiral galaxy—called that because if you could look down on it from above, it would look like a gigantic pinwheel, with great, outstretched arms extending from its center. The solar system and our planet are located in one of the swirling arms— about 26,000 light years from the center of the Galaxy. Everything in the Galaxy swirls around the center, and it takes 250 million years for our solar system, riding in the spiral arm, to make one complete revolution.

Other types of galaxies also exist. Elliptical galaxies have an oval shape, something like a football (but a little less pointed), with no spiral arms. Some are rounder, and some look more like a cigar. A few galaxies do not fit a category— their shapes are irregular and unclassifiable. These are known as irregular galaxies, and they often have a satellite relationship with another, larger, galaxy.

All the stars and other objects are held together within a galaxy by gravity. Galaxies also form groups, or clusters, clumping together and leaving vast expanses of space where nothing rules except for dust particles and gases. The Milky Way is part of such a cluster, named the Local Group—although it does not seem very local from the human point of view. The name serves as an ironic reminder of the enormity of the universe, when we think of this huge cluster of many galaxies as "local." The Local Group consists of about 30 galaxies spread across a distance of about 3 million light years. One might ask, What, then, is long distance?

Stars

Stars come in many ages, sizes, colors, and degrees of brightness. New stars are constantly forming in regions thick with gas and dust, sweeping up matter and holding it together through the force of gravity. As they grow larger and hotter, these balls of hot gas get their heat and luminosity from a process known as thermonuclear fusion, during which hydrogen atoms are fused together to form helium atoms, causing a huge release of energy. During the course of its long lifetime, a star passes through many life changes. Once fusion begins, the star begins to stabilize and become a medium star like our Sun. Later, as it grows older, it begins to run out of hydrogen fuel, and it grows larger, becoming a red giant. It may end its days in the spectacular explosion of a supernova or just run out of fuel eventually and become a tiny, faint white dwarf.

Astronomers are especially intrigued by an object called a *black hole,* which is a formerly massive star that has collapsed in on itself due to the force of its own gravity. Black holes exert a huge gravita-tional pull—and nothing ever escapes, not even light. Another mysterious object, known as a *quasar,* gives off a tremendous amount of energy—some quasars are a trillion times brighter than our Sun. Scientists think that quasars may generate their energy from huge black holes located at the center of galaxies. Even though quasars are very bright and huge—many are as big as our solar system—they cannot be seen with the naked eye because they are so old and so far away, up to billions of light years distant from Earth. Their name means "quasi-stellar radio source," meaning "starlike emitters of radio waves," but they actually give off more radiation in other portions of the electromagnetic spectrum—including *infrared waves, ultraviolet radiation, X rays,* and *gamma rays.*

Neutron stars are stars that have collapsed inward with such force that their molecules have become packed densely together in a neutron core. Neutron stars spin very rapidly, emitting radio waves. Radio waves with a definite pulse have been collected from some neutron stars, which have gained the name of "pulsars."

Astronomers delight in the diversity of these objects that form the universe. Many, such as black holes and a mysterious substance known as dark matter, may hold secrets about the formation of the universe and its evolution. All the objects represent great puzzles, riddles to work out to solve the mysteries of nature.

By 1956 the National Radio Astronomy Observatory (NRAO) was founded in Green Bank, West Virginia. Nestled in a green valley and shielded by mountains to the east and west, the location is ideal for radio astronomy. By 1959 Green Bank's first radio telescope was completed, an antenna that was 85 feet (26 m) in diameter. The big 300-foot (91.5-m) telescope began surveying the skies in 1962 and continued to do so until it collapsed in 1988. A third telescope, a 140-foot (43-m) antenna, was added in 1965. In 2000, the original large telescope was replaced by the Green Bank Telescope, the largest fully steerable radio telescope in the world, with a diameter of 345 feet (105 m).

Interest in radio astronomy was increasing, and the trend has never stopped. By 2002 the NRAO, now managed from Charlottesville, Virginia, has opened a total of three sites: the Green Bank Observatory; the Kitt Peak Observatory in Tucson, Arizona; and an interesting setup called the Very Large Array, built near Socorro, New Mexico, in 1980. The Very Large Array combines twenty-seven 82-foot (25-m) telescopes set up in a Y-shaped formation to create a giant antenna that can collect radio signals from far-distant objects. The combined telescope resolution is equivalent to a single 22-mile (36-km) antenna!

The world's largest fixed-dish antenna was built in 1963 and is actually a natural valley near Arecibo, Puerto Rico. The telescope dish measures 1,000 feet (300 m) across. The antenna consists of 40,000 individual reflecting panels attached to a network of steel cables. The panels focus incoming radio waves from objects in space onto a detecting platform suspended above the dish.

In the past 40 years, radio astronomers have found that all objects in the universe emit radio waves. Using the latest techniques and antennas, they can detect radio waves from most known

The largest object in this photo is the Robert C. Byrd Telescope (also known as the Green Bank Telescope), which is part of the National Radio Astronomy Observatory at Green Bank, West Virginia. The observatory collects radio waves from deep space, which scientists study to obtain information about galaxies, new stars, planets, and other celestial bodies.

objects, and these emissions provide another way of looking at the cosmos. Magnetic properties, in particular, can only be detected by radio astronomy.

In the beginning, radio astronomy offered several breakthrough discoveries—the existence of background radiation (left over from the so-called "big bang" from which most astronomers think the universe began), the presence of complex molecules in the regions between the stars, and the existence of radio galaxies. Radio astronomy also alerted astronomers and astrophysicists to the existence of two interesting types of objects: quasars and pulsars. Quasars are the most luminous objects in the universe, but they are very small—a fact confirmed through radio astronomy. Quasars also offer evidence of the existence of black holes. Pulsars form during a supernova—a cataclysmic explosion that ends the life of a massive star. After outer layers blow off into space, only a tiny collapsed core remains, usually spinning rapidly at first. At the beginning, pulsars spin so fast they emit radio signals, X rays, and other types of radiation. As the pulsar ages, it slows. Radio signals become weaker and finally they "turn off." In 2002 astronomers from the University of Manchester, England, used the two-year-old Green Bank Telescope in West Virginia. They found the youngest radio-emitting pulsar ever. It is only 820 years old, and it is located in the remnant of a supernova 10,000 light years away in the constellation Cassiopeia. Astronomers hope to monitor the pulsar and learn a lot about the early development of these mysterious objects.

X Rays from the Universe

Radio signals from space were a natural beginning to exploration of nonvisual astronomy. Radio signals easily penetrate Earth's atmosphere. However, X rays do not. They are easily absorbed. Astronomers and astrophysicists suspected that X rays were given off by objects in space, though—especially the Sun. Evidence in Earth's lower ionosphere—about 30 miles (50 km) above the surface—showed effects that tipped them off. Scientists at the U.S. Naval Research Laboratory sent a sounding rocket up in 1949 with experiments onboard that confirmed the presence of X rays. They assumed that probably other

As you have seen, visible light makes up only a small portion of the electromagnetic spectrum. So using only instruments that work with visible light would be like trying to find your way out of a forest with your eyes closed, earplugs in your ears, a gag over your mouth so you couldn't taste anything, and a clothespin on your nose. You would be left with the sense of touch and that's all. In recent years, scientists have made a point of exploring the universe in every segment of the electromagnetic spectrum they can.

Radio waves are electromagnetic waves having much longer wavelengths than visible light. In 1932, when Karl Jansky discovered radio waves coming from an astronomical object, many people were surprised. As it turns out, a lot of astronomical objects emit radio waves. However, radio waves need to be collected differently from light waves. Astronomers began developing systems that allow them to make graphs, or pictures from the radio waves emitted by astronomical objects.

How does a star or other astronomical object send off radio waves? Several processes produce radio waves, including thermal (or heat) radiation from planets and other solid bodies, thermal radiation from hot gas in the interstellar medium, and pulsed radiation caused when neutron stars rotate through the intense magnetic field and energetic electrons that surround them.

Solar flares and sunspots, in particular, have turned out to be strong sources of radio emission. Scientists have studied them extensively and have recorded extensive data from sunspot and flare activity—with great success. The complex processes that take place near the Sun's surface are now better understood, and scientists have been able to set up an advance warning system for Sun flares, which can damage unprotected satellites and electronic equipment, as well as interrupting radio communications on the ground. Radio telescopes have also been trained on the planets and used to measure surface temperatures. They have also picked up radio emissions from Jupiter and have discovered an internal heating source within all four of the gas giants, Jupiter, Saturn, Uranus, and Neptune. Radio waves have also been picked up from binary stars and X-ray stars, supernova remnants, and magnetic fields in the interstellar regions.

Clouds above planets and gas and dust in space do not interfere much with radio transmissions, so radio astronomers have been able to obtain clearer pictures of stars and galaxies. By using a spectrometer, they have identified some 100 molecules in space, including many organic compounds such as methanol, ammonia, ethanol, and formaldehyde, in addition to water vapor and carbon dioxide. Increasing sophistication has steadily broadened the uses of radio astronomy, and by teaming optical and radio telescopes to study the sky, astronomers have greatly increased their ability to understand what is going on in the universe.

The bright object in this image is a quasar, one of the most unusual objects to be found in deep space. Scientists now believe that quasars are the very bright centers of distant galaxies. The brightness is probably due to the release of energy caused by the presence of a supermassive black hole.

stars besides the Sun gave off X rays, too. However, in 1949, before the space age, they had no way to detect X rays from sources located so far away.

Once astronomers had a chance to launch satellites to check the evidence from space, they found the entire universe glows with X rays. Human eyes just can't see them, but the space observatory instruments could. Soon, the astronomers' tools began to multiply and the entire

Grote Reber: Backyard Radio Astronomer

When Grote Reber (1911–2002) was still in high school, he became an amateur ("ham") radio operator. (No one is quite sure where the expression "ham radio" came from, but it refers to a short-wave radio operated by a licensed amateur.) Later, Reber attended the Illinois Institute of Technology and became a radio engineer, but that didn't end his amateur days. He read about Jansky's discoveries of radio emissions from the center of the Galaxy and he decided to do some radio astronomy on his own. So, in 1937 he built an antenna in his own backyard. The telescope wasn't small, at least not for his backyard. The bowl-shaped antenna measured 31 feet (9.4 m) in diameter. He used it to reveal discrete radio sources in the sky and to map the radio emissions he found. Reber found a job working for the National Bureau of Standards from 1947 to 1951, and he worked at the NRAO from 1957 to 1961. In between the two jobs, he did radio astronomy atop the extinct volcano Haleakala on the island Maui in Hawaii and also in Tasmania, Australia. In 1961 he went back to Tasmania, where he continued to explore the skies using radio astronomy. Today the telescope he built in his backyard in 1937 stands on display at the Green Bank Observatory, along with the straight-line antenna used by Karl Jansky to make his first important discovery.

Grote Reber poses next to a radio telescope. Using a radio telescope he built himself in the backyard of his home in Wheaton, Illinois, Reber made the first surveys of radio waves from space.

electromagnetic spectrum became part of the toolbox. By looking at astronomical objects in several different ways, their true nature began to emerge in a way that had never before been possible. It was a momentous revolution in the astronomical world.

These powerful telescopes at the Roque de los Muchacos Observatory on La Palma, one of the Canary Islands off the west coast of Africa, sit above the clouds. The site is one of the best locations for space observation on Earth.

Chapter 3

Mountaintop Astronomy

A t the beginning of the twentieth century, most astronomers were still thinking in terms of whether a telescope should be a refractor or a reflector. No one yet realized how many other choices would arise in years to come. The 40-inch (1-m) Yerkes telescope at Williams Bay, Wisconsin was still the best—but the days of big refractors were winding to an end, and reflectors were getting bigger and bigger. New questions began to arise, such as: How big a piece of sky could a telescope capture at one time in a photograph? The big 200-inch (5.1-m) Hale reflector was the first clear-sky, high mountaintop telescope, and it could probe deeply, but not more than one degree wide. Its neighbor, though, a 48-inch (1.2-m) Oschin Schmidt telescope, could capture seven degrees square in a single photograph. It took 1,870 stunning plates in the 1950s for a sky survey sponsored by the National Geographic Society and Palomar Observatory. The set of plates continues to be a valuable source of information for scientists all over the world.

Bigger and Bigger

After World War II, astronomy began to boom. National telescopes became the rule—since national budgets were better equipped to finance the teams of telescopes beginning to be seen as the heart of a good observatory. By the 1970s, several new beauties were ready for "first light," the moment when a telescope opens its lenses and mirrors and swings into action for the first time. The new 150-inch (4-m) Mayall reflector at Kitt Peak, Arizona, was the first—in 1973. Several other big ones just under 157 inches (4 m) followed, around the world. The Anglo-Australian Telescope at Siding Spring Mountain in Australia was completed in 1974. The European Southern Observatory's ESO Telescope at La Silla, Chile, turned on in 1977 and was a joint project of six European nations, uniting the scientific community in a new and productive effort. At an altitude of 13,800 feet (4,200 m) above sea level, the Canada-France-Hawaii Telescope began operation on Hawaii's Mauna Kea mountain in 1979. It made an enormous improvement in astronomical seeing. Its altitude is such a great advantage that some astronomers like to call it the "first ground-based space telescope."

Three more mammoth telescopes opened up on Mauna Kea in the 1990s—the Keck I in 1993, Keck II in 1996, and one of the twin 320-inch (8.1-m) Gemini telescopes in 1999. (The other Gemini telescope is on a mountaintop in Chile called Cerro Pachón.) Keck I and II look more like big frameworks than telescopes. They have a huge segmented mirror that allows for the enormous light-gathering power it has. The Gemini telescopes, however, still have solid mirrors. Big vents

These are the telescope domes of the Keck I and Keck II observatories in Hawaii. Situated on the dormant volcano Mauna Kea, these twin telescopes are the largest optical telescopes in the world.

in their domes help equalize the temperature between the air inside the dome and the air outside.

Changes in the way telescopes are mounted have made some of these improvements possible. Also, mirrors are no longer made of glass, as a rule. Instead they are quartz or special lightweight ceramics. High mountain altitudes and specialized instruments make observations possible in other regions of the electromagnetic spectrum, such as gamma-ray, infrared, ultraviolet, and X-ray radiation.

Also, CCDs, or charge-coupled devices, provide possibilities for recording faint objects as well as a telescope with an aperture 10 times as large could detect. They can also be connected to computers for analysis and automated searches. Few professional astronomers of the twenty-first century spend long nights at a telescope eyepiece. Far more frequently, they view the skies at a television screen or review the results of the night's viewing the next morning on a computer screen.

Astronomy is one of the best areas in science for both participation and significant contributions by amateurs. Backyard telescopes and telescope parties can provide immense enjoyment for skywatchers of every age. The age-old tradition of watching the skies on a clear evening has lost none of its luster since the days of the Babylonians—and it has gained a lot. Today, telescopes range from small refractors from a toy store (better than Galileo's telescope, but not that satisfying) to bigger refractors, reflectors, and other types of telescopes. Amateurs frequently are the first to spot a

> By revolutionizing the design of amateur telescopes, John Dobson has done much to enable the untrained amateur to observe the universe. Dobson is the founder of a group called the Sidewalk Astronomers. The members build telescopes and set them up in public places, where they encourage passersby to take a look at the universe.

However, many amateur astronomers continue to peer through their telescopes in the night air of their backyards or favorite cloudless hillside. The adventure of sweeping the skies remains for both amateurs and professionals, and amateur astronomers continue to make important contributions to science. Many amateur astronomers have discovered comets, asteroids, novas, and supernovas. Backyard telescopes team with automated equatorial mounts and computer software to take some of the guesswork out of watching the skies. And no excitement is quite the same as the first view of the rings of Saturn through a telescope eyepiece.

Since October 1996, the twin Keck telescopes on Mauna Kea in Hawaii have become the largest reflecting telescopes in the world.

new comet or near-Earth asteroid. The Hale-Bopp Comet was discovered independently by two amateur astronomers, Alan Hale and Thomas Bopp in July 1995. One was attending a star party, and the other, in a neighboring state, had gone to a favorite spot in the hills near his home.

Amateur astronomers come from every walk of life—from clinical psychologists to high school students, and from barefoot philosophers to grocery clerks. John Dobson probably comes under the "barefoot philosopher" category, and he may have done more for amateur astronomy around the world than any other single individual. Dobson, who was 84 in May 2000, designed a telescope that people could make, including grinding the mirror. It is inexpensive, easily portable, and large—with diameters from 12 to 20 inches (30 to 50 cm)—and it has caught on with many amateur astronomers. Dobson has taught his craft for over 30 years, and started an amateur astronomy club in the San Francisco Bay Area. Its name became the "Sidewalk Astronomers," bringing amateur astronomy to the city streets. Dobson, his long, gray ponytail swishing across his back, holds gatherings in city and national parks, talks astronomy, and teaches telescope making with great energy and enthusiasm—and also with a demanding insistence on perfection. Behind his tattered clothes he hides a sophistication and intelligence that are hard to miss. By 2000 his Sidewalk Astronomy idea had spread to the urban streets of many other countries, and the Dobsonian telescope had become known worldwide for its simple yet effective design. He is the ultimate amateur astronomer.

Each telescope's primary mirror is a giant 400 inches, or 33 feet (10 m), in diameter. With this enormous increase, Keck I and II can gather in four times as much light as the Hale telescope. In fact, each can gather in 17 times as much light as the Hubble Space Telescope! They can also see farther than the Hubble—but not as clearly.

Refracting telescopes are still very popular with amateurs, but as observatory telescopes got bigger, fewer and fewer were refractors. Large glass lenses are much heavier than mirrors, and they are more difficult to make free of defects. The largest refractor in the world remains the telescope at Yerkes Observatory. It has been in operation for a long time—since 1897.

The *Hubble Space Telescope* is about to detach from the space shuttle after a successful repair mission by the shuttle's astronauts. *Hubble* has provided astronomers with unprecedented looks into the deepest regions of space.

Chapter 4

The First Orbiting Observatories

A n astronomer's work has traditionally been lonely and cold. Astronomers have built observatories high on mountaintops, as you have seen. They have always tried to find the darkest skies, far from the city lights. They try to place their telescopes as high as possible in Earth's atmosphere. They may spend long nights alone at a telescope, waiting for clouds to clear. Often, a long-awaited event—for example, a moon crossing the face of a planet (a transit) or an eclipse—may not to be visible at all. No wonder astronomers began to dream of having a telescope in space, where no city lights or clouds or shimmering atmosphere interfered.

Seeing from Space: An Astronomer's Dream

The regions of space beyond Earth's atmosphere are different. All types of radiation travel through the vacuum of space at the speed of light. There are no clouds. There are no competing lights, except light from celestial objects, including the Sun's direct light and its light reflected by the Moon and Earth. There is no atmospheric turbulence in orbit. Just the vast vacuum and darkness of space.

As early as 1923, pioneer rocket engineer Hermann Oberth (1894–1989) of Transylvania, Romania, put forth the idea of a space-based telescope in a popular science book. A few decades later, in 1946, American astronomer Lyman Spitzer (1914–1997) wrote a paper that expanded on the idea. Beside the advantages for observation, he noted that the distortion of a telescope's optics by the pull of *gravity* would also not be a problem in a space telescope. He suggested using both small and large telescopes. Smaller telescopes—with diameters about 16.5 feet (5 m)—could examine dust and gases in the areas between the stars (*interstellar* regions). They could also find out what stars are made of. Larger telescopes—between about 16.5 and about 50 feet (5–15 m)—could find out more about some of the universe's mysterious objects, such as globular clusters and galaxies. Perhaps they could also measure the size of the universe.

Spitzer was a visionary—a serious one. He proposed having a major study done of these possibilities, in a report written more than 10 years before the first satellite was put in *orbit!* Most people at that time thought rockets and spaceships were only vague possibilities that might perhaps take place in the far-distant future. Some even believed they were no more real than the science fiction stories they saw at the movies.

Why a Telescope in Space?

Since the time of Galileo, telescopes have revolutionized astronomy. Bigger and better telescopes on the mountaintops of the world helped astronomers see much farther and more clearly than ever before. In the 400 years since telescopes were first invented, astronomers used them to make enormous discoveries about the solar system and the rest of the universe.

Yet ground-based telescopes—those that reside on Earth's surface—have four frustrating problems: Earth's cloud cover, the turbulence of the atmosphere, the inability of some forms of radiation to penetrate the atmosphere, and light pollution. Also, ground-based telescopes are restricted to nighttime use—the objects of astronomical observation "disappear" during daylight hours.

Cloudy Skies. If you've ever wanted to see an eclipse of the Moon on a cloudy night, you know how frustrating clouds can be for any astronomer. Behind that veil of clouds you know that exciting events are taking place, and yet there's nothing you can do but wait and hope the skies clear before the excitement is over. Imagine how unhappy you would be if you were an astronomer and the night arrived when you were scheduled to use one of the few big telescopes that could do your kind of work. And then it turned out to be a cloudy night!

The Shimmer of Atmosphere. Remember the little rhyme you learned as a kid? "Twinkle, twinkle, little star . . ." Well, twinkling stars are charming, but when you're trying to make out details—how big, how luminous, their positions, and what is around them—that shimmering

Infrared astronomy had begun in the 1960s with telescopes lifted high into the upper atmosphere by balloons. Small telescopes were carried above the lower atmosphere by Learjets and sounding rockets in the 1970s. In 1974, NASA came up with another ingenious method for observing in the infrared region of the spectrum: the *Kuiper Airborne Observatory (KAO)*. The observatory was really just a converted cargo plane made into a research platform. The big modified version of the Air Force C-141A was fitted with a cavity equipped to hold a telescope cooled by liquid helium. As many as six to ten researchers could fly aboard the plane, overseeing the data collection for their projects. The pilot swung through a high-altitude flight pattern planned to ascend above cloud cover to obtain views of specific targets in the heavens. Meanwhile, the researchers used computers and a finely tuned joystick to point the telescope and capture images of the objects they wanted to study. This flying platform did not provide the crystal-clear view a spaceborne observatory could have, but it was a good compromise, ascending as high as 45,000 feet (14 km). Traveling as far as 6,000 nautical miles in a single night's work, it provided useful research flights for infrared astronomers over the next twenty years. The *KAO* retired in 1995.

Its replacement, the *Stratospheric Observatory for Infrared Astronomy (SOFIA)*, is expected to begin flights in 2004. NASA is working with the German Aerospace Center (DLR) to modify a Boeing 747SP aircraft that will carry a 98-inch (2.5-m) reflecting telescope—giving *SOFIA* a much larger telescope and much more sensitive technology than the *KAO*. It will be the largest airborne observatory in the world and will outdo even the largest and highest ground-based telescopes.

and twinkling makes the job extra difficult. The cause is the constant turbulence of Earth's atmosphere, the layer of gases that lies like a protective blanket over our planet's surface.

Even on a mountaintop, the atmosphere's agitation causes blurry and indistinct images. Scientists have learned a lot of tricks with improved optics and computerized image processing. They can make up for a lot of this problem, but they can't compensate for it completely.

Blocked Radiation. We need Earth's atmosphere for survival. It is our shield against high-energy radiation from the Sun. Yet, that same blocking action is the astronomer's enemy. Astronomers have discovered that they can learn a lot about the universe by looking at objects in other ways than just looking through an optical telescope (or capturing images with film or electronics). They want to see the many kinds of radiation put out by objects in the universe—throughout the range of the electromagnetic spectrum. However, even by using special instruments, scientists cannot observe the full range of radiation—because our atmosphere is blocking it out.

So certain types of radiation do not ever reach the ground. The chemical composition of Earth's atmosphere prevents infrared (IR) and ultraviolet (UV) energy from reaching the ground. Infrared radiation is absorbed by water vapor and carbon dioxide (CO_2) in the air. The same ozone in the upper atmosphere that protects us against the Sun's UV rays makes them almost impossible to detect from the ground. Air molecules scatter X rays and gamma rays, so they are not easily observed from below Earth's blanket of air. Astronomers had found ways to get around some of these problems by placing telescopes high on mountaintops, flying in high-altitude airplanes, or sending instruments up on balloons or sounding rockets, which stayed only briefly above the atmosphere. However, none of these methods worked very well.

Polluting the Darkness. Most people don't think of light as a kind of pollution. But for astronomers, the lights from city streetlights, stores, homes, and headlights all compete against the tiny, faint objects they are trying to observe. Even the atmosphere itself has a faint natural glow.

Escaping the Envelope

By 1957 the Union of Soviet Socialist Republics (USSR, or Soviet Union)—a nation comprised of Russia and several other countries in eastern Europe and central Asia—had placed a little satellite called *Sputnik* in orbit. The United States had been working on a satellite, too. The competition hurried the process, and within a few months, the United States also had completed and launched its own satellite, named *Explorer 1*. That was the beginning of a space race in which the two nations tried to outdo each other with satellite launches and other feats in space. The competition continued for the rest of the Cold War, a period of time after World War II when Western nations and Communist nations, including the USSR, competed for world approval. It was a time of turmoil and bitterness between the two groups of nations, with the United States and the USSR at the forefront. Many people feared that a nuclear war might break out, and the lack of cooperation often slowed progress. The period did not end until the USSR disbanded in 1989. However, strangely, early progress in space might never have happened so quickly if the Cold War had not prodded both nations into competition.

By 1958, U.S. President Dwight D. Eisenhower established the National Aeronautics and Space Administration (NASA) to develop and manage programs for exploring space. From 1958 to 1972, NASA managed the first U.S. programs that put humans in space—Project Mercury, which put the first astronauts in space; Project Gemini, which tested space maneuvers; and Project Apollo, which landed astronauts on the Moon and returned them to Earth. The Soviets had competing programs. At the same time, NASA and the USSR were also launching satellites for communications, weather reports, surveillance, and scientific purposes.

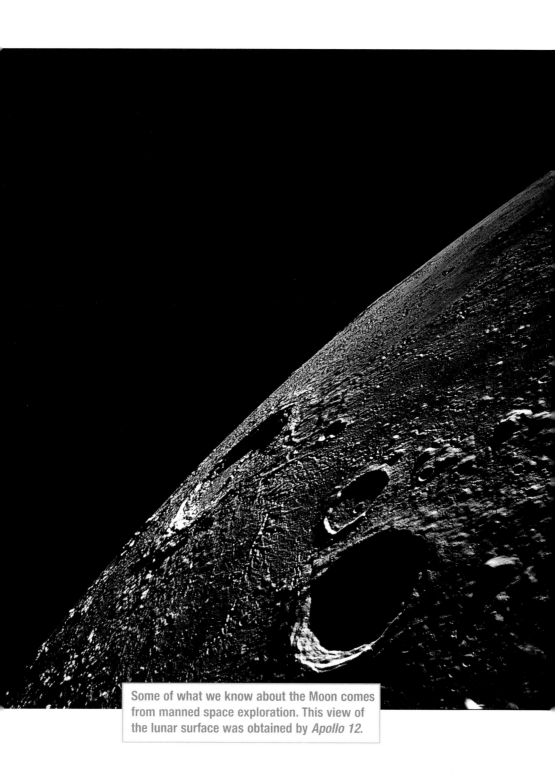

Some of what we know about the Moon comes from manned space exploration. This view of the lunar surface was obtained by *Apollo 12*.

By 1962—only five years after the Soviets launched *Sputnik*—the United Kingdom (UK) launched *Ariel 1*, the first of a series of six Ariel orbiting observatories. *Ariel 1* looked into solar UV and X-ray radiation and obtained an energy spectrum of primary cosmic rays. With that mission the space age began to make a whole new range of wavelengths available to astronomers. Progress was rapid and revolutionary—with the biggest strides at the ultraviolet, X-ray, and gamma-ray wavelengths. In 1972, two U.S. astronomical instruments began to orbit, both part of a program known as the *Orbiting Astronomical Observatory (OAO)*. The first *OAO* was a platform carrying UV telescopes, photoelectric telescopes, and UV spectrometers. Orbiting in space, it was able to obtain images in the UV part of the spectrum, which is completely blocked out by Earth's atmosphere for ground-based observations. The first *OAO* obtained images from 1972–1973. Another *OAO* telescope, called *Copernicus*, was also placed in orbit in 1972. Its main mirror was 32 inches (80 cm) in diameter, and it carried 4 X-ray telescopes and a UV telescope. The Copernicus mission lasted nine years, from 1972 to 1981. Others soon followed.

Ultraviolet Views: *IUE*

Ultraviolet astronomy can reveal secrets about every object in the universe—from a planet to a moon, from an asteroid to a comet, and from a quasar to a galaxy. Even the material found between stars—in the interstellar medium—has been examined using UV astronomy. The interstellar medium turns out to be made of about the same material throughout the universe—yet it contains bubbles blown into it by strong stellar winds, similar to our solar wind.

By the late 1970s, the first major observatory was launched that was dedicated to exploring the universe in just one region of the electromagnetic spectrum. This observatory gave its full attention to UV radiation. It made great strides toward finding out more about UV radiation coming from objects everywhere in the universe. It was called the *International Ultraviolet Explorer (IUE)*, and in 1978 it began nearly two decades of UV observation. During that time, the *IUE* established a major database of UV sources and took more than 10,000 spectra of astronomical objects during its long lifetime.

The *IUE* was a three-way joint project managed by NASA; the Science and Engineering Research Council (SERC), now the Particle Physics and Astronomy Research Council (PPARC), in the United Kingdom (UK); and the European Space Agency (ESA). NASA provided the launch site, spacecraft, telescope, spectrographs, and one ground observatory (at Goddard Spaceflight Center). ESA provided the solar panels and the other ground observatory (near Madrid, Spain). The UK furnished four spectrograph television cameras used as detectors. The satellite was launched from Kennedy Space Center into geosynchronous orbit over the Atlantic Ocean in January 1978.

The ground observatories managed the spacecraft's operations, but they also acted as traditional observatory sites—except that the telescope was far out in space. For the first time, visiting astronomers could make real-time observations of UV spectra from a satellite. *IUE* had a quick response time—less than one hour—so scientists could change the schedule if something came up. *IUE* made observations of all kinds of objects, from comets to quasars, and investigators learned a lot from its output.

Twentieth-Century Space Telescopes

Vital Statistics

Telescope	Dates of Operation	Description
Orbiting Astronomical Observatory (OAO)	1972–1973	Carried UV telescopes, photoelectric telescopes, and UV spectrometers
Copernicus	1972–1981	Part of the *OAO* series, carrying-X-ray and UV telescopes
International Ultraviolet Explorer (IUE)	1978–1996	Established a major record of UV sources and took more than 10,000 spectra of objects in its long lifetime
Infrared Astronomical Satellite (IRAS)	1983	First satellite built to do a major survey at infrared wavelengths
Roentgen Satellite (ROSAT)	1992–2001	German X-ray satellite, also carried extreme UV instrument
Extreme Ultraviolet Explorer (EUVE)	1992–2001	Detailed look at the extreme UV sky
Infrared Space Observatory (ISO)	1995–1997	A European supplement and replaement for *IRAS*

IUE lasted a long time—nearly 19 years. However, in 1996, it was time to vent its gases, drain its batteries, and turn off its transmitter. It had done its job well, and as of 1998, some 3,585 publications had been published using *IUE* results.

In the meantime, another UV observatory had launched in 1992, the *Extreme Ultraviolet Explorer (EUVE)*, a NASA project to explore the extreme ultraviolet (EUV) region of the spectrum—a new tool for astronomy. It continued to orbit until 2001.

IRAS: Unlocking Infrared Secrets

The *Infrared Astronomical Satellite (IRAS)* was launched in January 1983. It became the first satellite to survey the skies in the infrared portion of the electromagnetic spectrum. It carried a 24-inch (60-cm) Ritchey-Chrétien Cassegrain telescope with infrared detectors located at its focus. It was a joint project of NASA, the Netherlands, and Great Britain, and it made exciting contributions to the study of star formation and the examination of the center of the Milky Way. It also found many comets.

Unfortunately, *IRAS* had only ten months in orbit because the liquid helium it needed to cool the telescope and its detectors was slowly leaking from its tank. Finally *IRAS* was shut down November 21, 1983. Two years later, in November 1995, ESA launched a replacement observatory, the *Infrared Space Observatory (ISO).* It operated for nearly two years and collected even more data.

This view of deep space, called the Hubble Deep Field, is the "deepest-ever view" of the universe. This is a view all the way to the visible horizon of the universe.

Chapter 5

NASA's "Great Observatories" in Space

S oon after the first *Orbiting Astronomical Observatory* was launched in 1972, the U.S. National Aeronautics and Space Administration (NASA) began to make plans for something much bigger, a real observatory. The program was approved in 1977. With the successes of the early observatories, those plans began to grow. Within a few years, NASA had plans for five or more spaceborne observatories, several carrying multiple instruments. These astronomy platforms in space became known as the Great Observatories. By 1990, Spitzer's entire

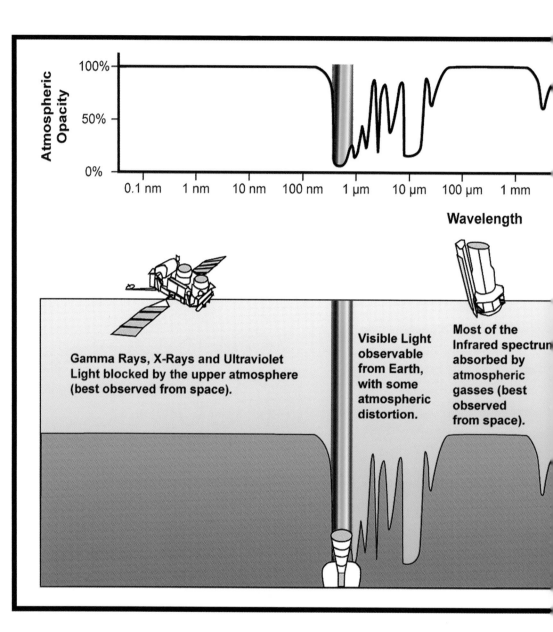

Atmospheric Opacity

100%
50%
0%

0.1 nm   1 nm   10 nm   100 nm   1 µm   10 µm   100 µm   1 mm

Wavelength

Gamma Rays, X-Rays and Ultraviolet Light blocked by the upper atmosphere (best observed from space).

Visible Light observable from Earth, with some atmospheric distortion.

Most of the Infrared spectrum absorbed by atmospheric gasses (best observed from space).

vision was coming true, with the launch of a large, powerful telescope, boosted above the atmosphere—a satellite placed in orbit around Earth. The first of these to launch was the *Hubble Space Telescope.*

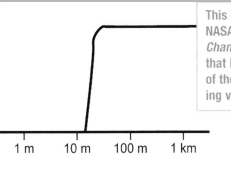

1 m   10 m   100 m   1 km

Radio Waves observable from Earth.

Long-wavelength Radio Waves blocked.

Hubble Space Telescope: Perseverance Pays Off

About the size of a school bus, the *Hubble Space Telescope* (*HST,* or *Hubble*) looks out into the darkness of space as it orbits 381 miles (613 km) above Earth. Like all the long term orbiting observatories, *Hubble* has no crew—it is a robot spacecraft, an electronic servant to humankind. *Hubble* is probably the most famous of all the space telescopes, and it has captured thousands of images that show details never before seen. It has recorded events that might otherwise have gone unseen, or at least not seen in the same way.

The path to this success was neither smooth nor easy, though. *Hubble* was all set to go, ready to be launched in 1986. Then on January 28, 1986, the unthinkable happened. The space shuttle *Challenger* exploded less than two minutes after liftoff and its pieces plunged into the Atlantic Ocean. Every member of its seven-person crew was killed. A thorough presidential investigation took place to find out why the explosion occurred. The problem was soon uncovered. A faulty O-ring between segments of solid-fuel rockets had become brittle in the bitter-cold winter weather. The brittleness kept it from keeping its seal, and fuel escaped. It caught fire, and the explosion ensued. NASA had to do a lot of reorganizing to put improved safety checks in place to make sure that such an accident would not happen again. In the meantime, all space shuttle orbiters were grounded for more than 18 months.

When space shuttle launches began again, *Hubble* had to wait its turn. Finally, the space telescope was launched aboard the space shuttle *Discovery* on April 24, 1990. High hopes swelled among astronomers and the public. The pictures from *Hubble* should be awesome. However, as the first pictures came in, excitement turned to disappointment. They were blurry. Something was wrong.

An examination of the records revealed that an error had been made in grinding the main mirror. *Hubble* had been sitting on the ground waiting for four extra years, and the problem could easily have been fixed, but because of a flaw in the testing, the grinding error was not detected until *Hubble* was orbiting Earth. Yet *Hubble* is a success story. Resourceful engineers and scientists figured out a way to overcome the flaw in the mirror by installing a corrective camera to compensate. In 1993 a crew of shuttle astronauts reeled in the satellite from its orbit and repaired it in the cargo bay of the shuttle. The crew's doctoring was a success. The field of vision was not as wide, but the optics were greatly improved. Shuttle crews have gone back to *Hubble* three times since then—in 1997, 1999, and 2002—to update computers, cameras, and instruments; replace aging or faulty parts; and update the power supply. Their doctoring has greatly lengthened the expected lifetime of *HST*.

Hubble's exciting images have provided new clues to the size of the universe and have shown that about 50 billion more galaxies exist in the universe than anyone thought before. This discovery makes the

This is the nucleus of a galaxy in the constellation Circinus. The bright spot at the center is the Seyfert nucleus, the indication of the presence of a supermassive black hole at the center of the galaxy.

The Crab Nebula, seen here in a Hubble photograph, is the best-known supernova remnant. A supernova remnant is a huge cloud of gas created by the explosion of a star at the supernova stage.

telescope's name especially appropriate, since it was named after the astronomer Edwin Powell Hubble (1889–1953). Hubble, who worked at the Mount Wilson Observatory in California, was the first to show that galaxies exist beyond our own Milky Way. *HST* has also con-

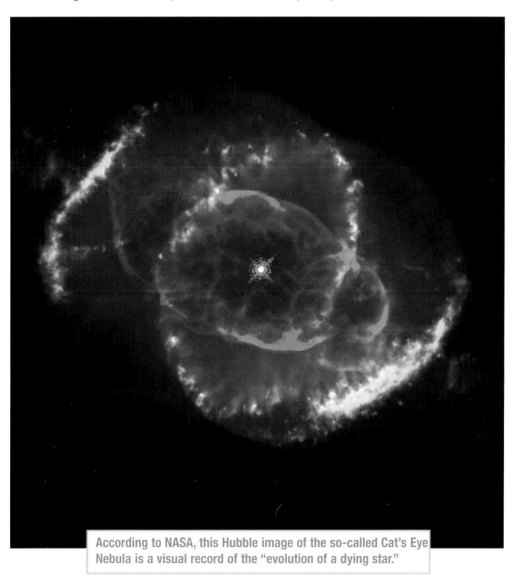

According to NASA, this Hubble image of the so-called Cat's Eye Nebula is a visual record of the "evolution of a dying star."

Not everyone knows exactly what career path to take at the outset. Deborah Levine had so many different interests that she had a hard time deciding what her major was in college. Should she pursue writing? Psychology was fascinating. Horses were a delight. Theater was promising. Finally, she had to decide, and she settled on physics, which she liked a lot. She received her bachelor of science degree in physics from the University of North Carolina at Chapel Hill and also, later, a master of science degree in physics. However, when she began work on her Ph.D. she realized that she couldn't imagine writing a dissertation in physics. A dissertation usually describes original research—exploring a topic in a way that has not been covered previously by anyone else. Levine says she realized that a dissertation required a higher level of interest than her "I kind of like this stuff" relationship with physics.

So she took a couple of years off from school and worked for Boeing in Seattle as an infrared engineer. Later, she helped astronomers use the data from *IRAS*. After about a year as an astronomers' research aide, or "Superfriend," as she was called, she decided to move into their ranks. As she puts it, "I decided that I really wanted my own 'license to practice astronomy.'" She began the graduate program in astronomy at UCLA while still working 20 to 40 hours a week. She earned her Ph.D. in 1995 and almost right away she received the job of U.S. Liaison Astronomer for the *Infrared Space Observatory (ISO)* at the ESA observatory in Spain.

"There," she says, "I discovered what I am really good at—figuring out how the puzzle of science operations for an observatory fits together!" She was able to observe how the science operations teams for *ISO* worked together and what kinds of coordination are needed to take place to make everything run smoothly and to make good data available to the astronomers who are using the instruments.

When she returned to the United States, she became Task Lead for all four science operations teams for *SIRTF*, an Earth-orbiting infrared observatory like *ISO*. And she loves the job's complexities and challenges.

When she isn't working, she can be found at the riding club next door to the Jet Propulsion Laboratory where she works in Pasadena, California. She does competition riding with her horse, Clifton Smint. She also works in a therapeutic riding program for children who have mental, social, and physical disabilities. "I find that working with these children," she says, "who are exactly who they are without pretension and who take the world very much as it comes, helps to keep me focused on what is really important in life . . . . And besides that, it's fun!"

firmed that *black holes* really do exist. A black hole is a celestial body with such great surface gravity that light cannot escape from it.

The *Hubble Space Telescope* became known for its remarkable photos of vastly distant objects, as well as nearby objects in our solar system. By mid-2002, *Hubble* had taken some 420,000 exposures since its launch in 1990, and it had observed 17,000 astronomical sights. Its output had also yielded some 3,200 scientific papers. NASA plans to bring HST home aboard the shuttle in 2010, after its replacement, the *Next Generation Space Telescope (NGST),* has taken over. The *NGST* was renamed the *James Webb Space Telescope* (*JWST*) in 2002 to honor James E. Webb, NASA's second administrator. *HST* will go on display at the Smithsonian Institution in Washington, DC.

Compton Gamma-Ray Observatory (CGRO)

Another satellite, the *Compton Gamma-Ray Observatory (CGRO),* carried four large "telescopes," some as large as a compact car. Each one recognized gamma rays within a specific energy range. Gamma rays, like all radiation, can only be detected when they interact with matter. *CGRO* detectors converted the rays to flashes of visible light. Then these flashes of light were counted and measured. Gamma rays produce the highest energy radiation in the electromagnetic spectrum— from tens of thousands to tens of billions of electron volts, or eV. (Visible light produces only a few eVs, by contrast.) Cosmic gamma rays cannot be detected at all on Earth because they can't penetrate the atmosphere. But many of the most interesting objects discovered in the past few decades, including quasars, pulsars, and neutron stars, involve large releases of energy that produce gamma rays. Astronomers

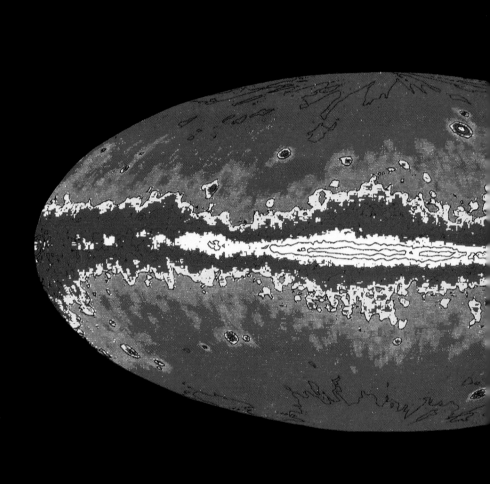

This is a colored gamma-ray map of the whole sky. The horizontal band at the center is the Milky Way. The white spots along it are pulsars, or rapidly spinning neutron stars. The other bright spots are probably quasars.

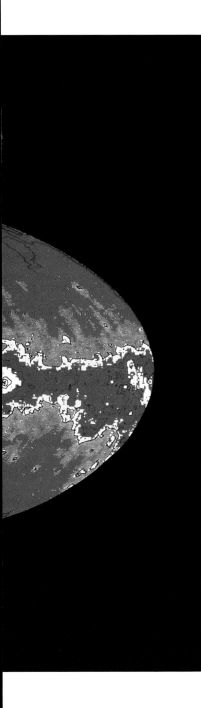

found they gained insights on the nature of these objects, their structures, and their dynamics from *CGRO.*

CGRO, named after Nobel prize-winning physicist Arthur Holly Compton, was launched aboard the space shuttle *Atlantis* on April 5, 1991. All went smoothly and *Atlantis* headed for the orbit at 450 mi (724 km) where *CGRO* would be released to start its work. As the crew members prepared to set the heavy, 17-ton spacecraft free, though, the high-gain antenna got stuck. This antenna was required for the observatory's mission. Its purpose was to send information to the communications satellite, which would in turn send it to the ground stations. Without it, *CGRO* would be crippled. The crew performed an emergency space walk and got the antenna unstuck, and *CGRO* began its voyage.

The mission lasted nine years. Finally, a necessary gyroscope gave signs of failing and NASA engineers began planning where and when to bring the big bird down safely, while they still had good control. On June 4, 2000, *CGRO* reentered

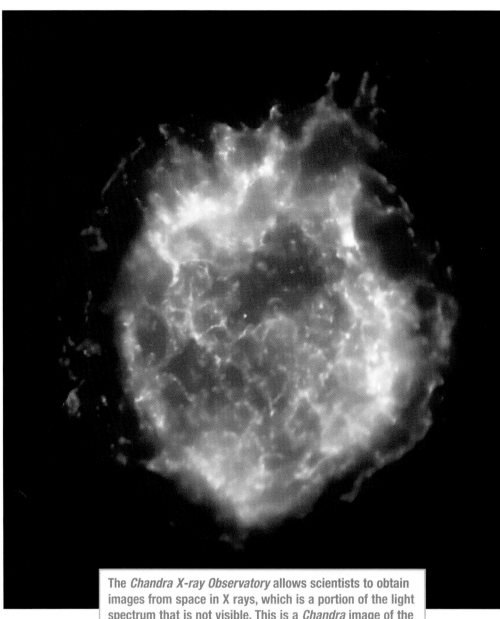

The *Chandra X-ray Observatory* allows scientists to obtain images from space in X rays, which is a portion of the light spectrum that is not visible. This is a *Chandra* image of the remnant of the supernova known as Cassiopeia A.

the atmosphere and those pieces that survived reentry broke up as planned and plunged safely into the Pacific Ocean some 2,500 miles (4,000 km) southeast of Hawaii.

Chandra X-Ray Observatory (CXO)

Perhaps NASA's most exciting observatory to date is the *Chandra X-Ray Observatory*, named after Indian-American theoretical physicist Subrahmanyan Chandrasekhar (1910–1995), better know as "Chandra." Launched in 1999, the *Chandra X-Ray Observatory* has delivered brilliant images and many discoveries—including the first full view of a blast wave from an exploding star, a flare emitted by a brown dwarf, and a small galaxy being consumed by a larger one.

Only two months after its launch from the space shuttle, the observatory showed that a brilliant ring exists around the center of the Crab Pulsar. Located in the Crab Nebula, the pulsar is the collapsed remains of a massive star gone supernova. The ring provided clues to scientists about how the pulsar energizes the entire nebula.

Astronomers know that a massive black hole exists at the center of our Milky Way Galaxy, but they have never found the X-ray emission they expect from that region. *Chandra* has found a faint X-ray source near the center of the Milky Way Galaxy that may be the long-sought sign.

Chandra also found that a gas funnel pouring into a huge black hole two million light years away turns out to be much cooler than scientists expected. As Harvey Tananbaum, astronomer and director of the Chandra X-Ray Science Center, remarked, "*Chandra* is teaching us to expect the unexpected about all sorts of objects ranging from comets in our solar system and relatively nearby brown dwarfs to distant black holes billions of light years away."

What happens when two galaxies the size of our own Milky Way collide? In its best image yet of colliding galaxies, *Chandra* showed in 2000 that a lot happens. Since many such mergers have very likely happened, even in our own Galaxy, the information probably holds insights about how the universe came to look as it does today. From *Chandra*'s evidence, scientists think that vast numbers of new stars have formed as a result of a giant merger in the galaxy called Arp 220. The merger also sent vast shock waves through the intergalactic regions of space. Possibly, an enormously massive black hole may also be forming at the center of the merged galaxy. From *Chandra*'s information, astronomers conclude that the merger has been taking place for some 10 million years, making it a recent event in cosmic terms. Scientists think of the events taking place in Arp 220 as similar to events that were probably common when the universe first formed, and as usual the information coming from *Chandra* is keeping them guessing.

Space Infrared Telescope Facility (SIRTF)

SIRTF, to be launched in August 2003, will pick up where *IRAS* and *ISO* left off, examining the infrared region of the spectrum. It is the last planned addition to the Great Observatories (not counting the *James Webb Space Telescope*). Recent advances in technology should make this observatory one of the greatest and most productive ever.

Astronomers sometimes refer to the 1990s as the "Decade of the Infrared" because *IRAS* and *ISO* made so many important contributions. *SIRTF* should be able to map large, complex areas with its advanced

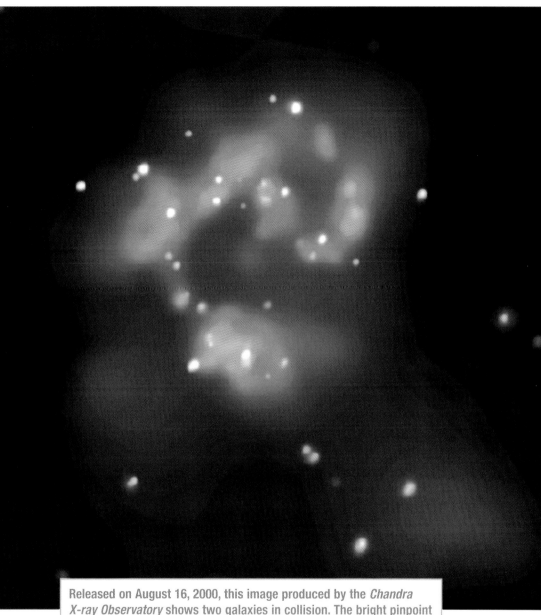

Released on August 16, 2000, this image produced by the *Chandra X-ray Observatory* shows two galaxies in collision. The bright pinpoint objects of light are black holes pulling gas from nearby stars.

Nasa's Great Observatories

Vital Statistics

Telescope	Launch Date	Description
Hubble Space Telescope (HST)	1990; mission extended to 2010	To cover visible-light astronomy, as well as near infrared and ultraviolet portions of the spectrum
Compton Gamma Ray Observatory (CGRO)	1991; retired in 2000	To collect data from the most violent, extremely energetic physical processes in the universe
Chandra X-Ray Observatory (CXO)	1999	To observe such X-ray emitters as black holes, quasars, and high-temperature gases
Space Infrared Telescope (SIRTF)	2003 (planned)	To capture thermal infrared emissions blocked by the atmosphere; to orbit the Sun, trailing Earth
James Webb Space Telescope (JWST)	2011 (planned)	To pick up where *Hubble* leaves off

arrays of infrared detectors. It also should be able to measure spectra at a mind-boggling rate—one million times as fast as any other spaceborne infrared telescope. Astronomers expect *SIRTF* to open up new understanding of many key questions, including the formation of planets and stars, the origin of energetic galaxies and quasars, the distribution of matter and galaxies, and the formation and evolution of galaxies.

This photo from the space shuttle *Endeavour* shows what is known as Earth's *airglow*. From a spacecraft in orbit, one can see clearly the different layers of the atmosphere by looking toward the Sun before dawn or after sunset.

Chapter 6

Traveling Sightseers

Within our solar system, robot spacecraft have paid visits to every planet except Pluto, to the Moon (including human visitors), to the Sun, and to comets and asteroids—all within the last 50 years! These explorations have completely changed human understanding of its neighbors in space. Up until the first close-ups came in from Mars, many people believed that intelligent life might live there. No one had yet detected the rings of Jupiter, Uranus, and Neptune or seen what was beneath the clouds covering Venus.

The first astronomical satellite was *Ariel 1* launched by the UK in 1962 to study the Sun. Most visits to other parts of the solar system made in the early years were launched by the United States and the

Soviet Union. In the last 20 years, though, ESA, Japan, and the UK all have joined in on sending robot ambassadors to planets, moons, asteroids, and comets. The first efforts were experimental flybys—small spacecraft following a trajectory past an object for a few quick images, perhaps a few measurements with a UV spectrometer, and then the visit was over—much too quickly. More recently, some spacecraft have orbited their targets for months, even years—mapping with radar at Venus or swinging by Jupiter's four big moons for multiple passes, answering as many questions as possible about these vastly different worlds. Some spacecraft sent robot landers down to the surface to scoop up dirt and run tests or to trundle across the surface—the ultimate remote-control toy car. More trips are planned for the future. For planetary scientists, these have been exciting years. Many insights about the origins of our own planet and its history have come from these explorations, and many more will come in the future.

Planetary Explorers

In 1962 a little spacecraft called *Mariner 2* became the first visitor to another planet as it skimmed past Venus on August 27. Since then, dozens of other spacecraft have visited the planets. The United States has sent many specialized missions to Mars, Venus, and the Moon, as has the Soviet Union. One Mariner mission to Venus also made two visits to Mercury. In the 1970s and 1980s two Pioneer missions and two missions called Voyager from the United States made big tours through the outer solar system, swinging by Jupiter and Saturn. One *Voyager* also visited Uranus and Neptune to give curious humans their first close-up of these faraway gas giants and their moons. Spectacular

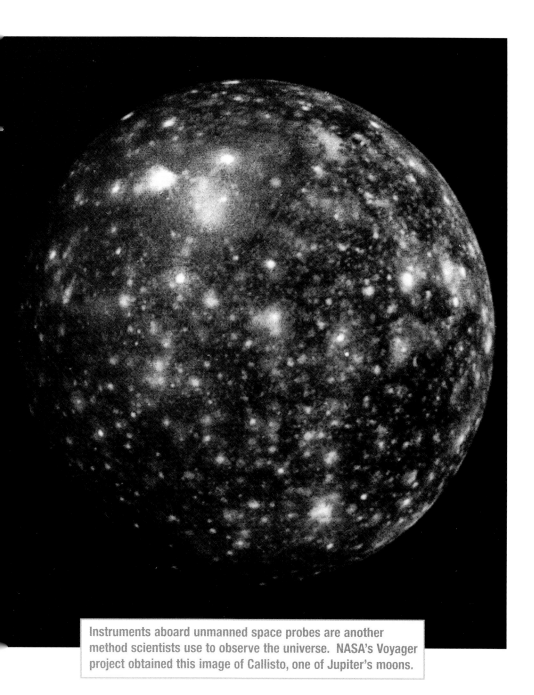

Instruments aboard unmanned space probes are another method scientists use to observe the universe. NASA's Voyager project obtained this image of Callisto, one of Jupiter's moons.

images transformed our vision of the outer solar system. More recent envoys have included *Galileo,* which spent nearly eight years visiting Jupiter and its biggest moons, and *Cassini,* a mission to Saturn and its big moon Titan. Thanks to many visits to Venus by Soviet and U.S. spacecraft in the 1960s, 70s, and 80s, we now know this planet is sizzling hot beneath clouds of poisonous gases—not the jungle paradise once imagined by science fiction writers. Two orbiters have mapped the surface of Mars in the 1990s and early twenty-first century, and in one month in the summer of 2003 three missions set off on their way to Mars. The United Kingdom's *Beagle 2* (named after Charles Darwin's ship) was designed to ride aboard another spacecraft also destined for Mars, the European Space Agency (ESA) spacecraft, *Mars Express.* Like *Beagle 2,* NASA's *Spirit* rover spacecraft is a lander, joining the international fleet to study Martian soil and rocks. *Mars Express* carries instruments for detecting water from orbit that may be hidden beneath the surface. Mars is the one planet that some scientists think may harbor signs of life—and finding water would make that exciting possibility much more likely. Future missions will spend more time studying Mercury and other planets and their moons. They may even visit Pluto and the Kuiper Belt beyond that faraway icy rock.

Visiting the Comets

Once a spacecraft is launched, sometimes investigators and engineers team up to find extra duties it can perform, once its job is done. That is exactly what happened to *ISEE-3* (*International Sun/Earth Explorer 3*), one of three solar observers launched in 1978. By 1982 its job of observing the solar wind and the relationship between Sun and Earth at the boundaries of Earth's magnetosphere was finished. So NASA

Against the backdrop of the constellation Orion, the Leonid meteor shower lights up the sky. The Leonid meteor shower is made up of bits and pieces that break off from Comet Tempel-Tuttle, which orbits the Sun every 33 years.

engineers retooled its trajectory and headed it off for a whole new life. Now dubbed *ICE* (*International Cometary Explorer*), this spacecraft became the first mission ever sent to observe a comet—and in fact, it observed not one but two comets. On June 5, 1985, *ICE* swung behind Comet Giacobini-Zinner at a distance of about 16,500 miles (26,550 km) and collected particles from the comet's tail to be analyzed by its instruments. Then on September 11, *ICE* collected its first data on the comet. It was the first time any mission had had the opportunity to study a comet and its surroundings on the spot. The spacecraft found a region where charged particles from the comet were interacting with particles from the solar wind. It also detected a tail about 15,500 miles (25,000 km) wide composed of plasma, a gas containing both positive and negative particles in almost complete balance. *ICE* also found water molecules and carbon monoxide ions—and that was confirmation of a theory that a comet is like a "dirty snowball." The spacecraft flew within 4,880 miles (7,862 km) of the comet on September 11, and, even though NASA engineers were worried, it suffered very little damage from the dust surrounding the nucleus. (This could have been a big problem, since *ICE* was never planned for such a mission and had no dust protection at all.)

The following year, *ICE* joined five other spacecraft from several nations in an internationally coordinated observation of Comet Halley. *ICE* made its observations on March 28, 1986, but could get no closer than 19 million miles (31 million km). Still, the spacecraft was able to collect data about the solar wind "upstream" from the comet. The most distant flyby of all the missions to Halley, *ICE* still made history with its flyby of Comet Giacobini-Zinner and did a job no one had imagined when the spacecraft was launched.

In 2014, *ICE* may return to Earth and NASA may try to bring the stalwart spacecraft back home. If that works, NASA has already promised the spacecraft to the Smithsonian Institution for exhibit.

The Soviet Union's Vega Missions

The Soviet Union (now Russia and several nearby countries) also restructured a pair of space missions already planned to visit Venus and sent them both to visit Comet Halley, as well. The spacecraft were designed much like the previous Soviet missions to Venus. *Vega 1* was launched December 15, 1984, with V*ega 2* following six days later, on December 21. They both arrived at Venus in June the following year. Each of these spacecraft had two parts: a flyby spacecraft to collect data and a balloon probe to study the atmosphere. The two balloons were released and descended into the thick atmosphere of Venus, where they both transmitted data until they were finally destroyed by the crushing atmospheric pressure.

After collecting data from the balloons, the two flyby spacecraft continued on to rendezvous with Comet Halley. *Vega 1* arrived first, beginning to take images as early as March 4, 1986, and making its closest approach on March 6, 1986. These images were used by the planners for *Giotto*, the European Space Agency's spacecraft, for planning its closest approach within a few days.

The first images from *Vega 1* showed two bright spots, and at first scientists thought that Comet Halley had a double nucleus. Later, though, the two bright spots turned out to be two jets of gas that were spewing dust and gases from the interior of the nucleus. The nucleus also looked dark in the images and the infrared spectrometer showed a nuclear temperature of 80–260°F (300–400 K)—surprisingly high for a small, icy body.

The Giotto mission was planned by the European Space Agency specifically for visiting comets—first comet Halley, and then *Giotto* would extend its mission to visit another one, Comet Grigg-Skjellerup, in 1992. For the Halley mission, *Giotto* took the first close-up images of a nucleus of a comet. It determined what elements and isotopes comprised the gases and dust of the coma. It explored the chemical and physical processes going on in the comet's atmosphere and ionosphere. It made measurements of the dust and gases. And it investigated the relationship between the plasma surrounding the comet and the solar wind.

Giotto was designed to go in closer to the comet nucleus than any of the other missions, and it came within 300 miles (482 km). At first, everything seemed to be going fine. The spacecraft began sending images to Earth. They showed that Halley was shaped like a peanut and had two jets spewing bright material. The dust impacts seemed minimal when suddenly, wham! The best guess is that the spacecraft crossed through one of the jets and got struck by a sizable dust particle that swung it out of position for communicating with Earth. Engineers worked for 30 minutes before they could get it lined up again. Some damage had been done, but *Giotto* had done a great job of collecting information just the same.

Giotto's information showed that the material Halley was throwing out into surrounding space was mostly water—about 80 percent by volume. The spacecraft found seven jets that among them were spewing some 3 tons of material per second. *Giotto* also provided data that showed that the surface was covered with a layer of organic material.

Twins from Japan

Japan also launched twin spacecraft. The second, *Suisei* (meaning "comet" in Japanese), launched on August 18, 1985, and began its observations of Halley first, in November 1985, before its twin reached the area. *Suisei* made observations of ultraviolet emissions from the comet—as many as six images each day up to its closest approach on March 8, 1986. Then *Suisei*'s UV instrument was turned off and the solar wind experiment began. *Suisei*, like *ICE*, also detected water and carbon monoxide, plus carbon dioxide ions. The spacecraft took a few hits, but succeeded in detecting several outbursts of jets from the comet as the comet turned on its axis.

The first of the twins, *Sakigake* (meaning "pioneer" in Japanese), lifted off January 7, 1985. Its goal was to measure the solar wind and magnetic field in the vicinity of Comet Halley, as it flew by. It came closest on March 11, 1986, but only at a distance of about 4.5 million miles (7 million km). *Sakigake* also helped act as a reference for *Giotto* as the ESA spacecraft prepared for its close approach.

Composite View

The Halley observations—coordinated by many countries and making use of several spacecraft—provided an exciting look at the famous Comet Halley. Edmond Halley had always encouraged international cooperation among scientists and pooling of resources. So it was fitting that his comet was the object of this unprecedented international space effort. Never before had so many countries cooperated in any space observation.

At the dawn of the twenty-first century, several new missions began the planning stages. One, *Deep Space 1*, has already completed its mission. *Deep Space 1*'s main purpose was to test a new propulsion system, but after that job was done, it made a risky detour to visit a comet named Borrelly. On the way, *Deep Space 1* had to dodge thick clouds of comet dust that could have ended its voyage. Then, traveling inside the comet's coma, it made its closest approach on September 22, 2001.

The images *Deep Space 1* sent back were the best yet, and the rest of its scientific data was also exciting. The spacecraft took black-and-white pictures, infrared measurements, data on ions and electrons, and measurements of the magnetic field and plasma waves around the comet. It explored the size of the comet, the nature of its surface, its brightness, its mass, and its density. It measured and identified the gases surrounding the comet, and measured the interaction of the solar wind with the comet.

Traveling to the Sun

In 1990, NASA launched a joint NASA/European Space Agency (ESA) spacecraft called *Ulysses* from the space shuttle *Discovery*. Once in Earth orbit, the spacecraft turned on its booster rockets and started on its way to a special orbit around the Sun—a path that would loop the spacecraft over the Sun's poles. This unusual orbit gave scientists a chance to survey areas of the Sun that they had never seen before.

Engineers knew that getting *Ulysses* to this special orbit was going to require some extra energy because the spacecraft would have to leave the orbital plane—the region through which the planets move around the Sun. In the fastest spacecraft launch ever, the 816-pound (370-kg) spacecraft traveled at a speed of 7 miles (11 km) per second as it left the realm controlled by Earth's gravity.

First, *Ulysses* headed for Jupiter—which sounds like the wrong direction! However, by looping past Jupiter, the spacecraft was able to gain an extra boost of speed, known as a "gravity assist." While in Jupiter's neighborhood, *Ulysses* studied the planet's magnetism and radiation. Then it sped on to begin its tour around the polar regions of the Sun.

As *Ulysses* swung by Jupiter, the spacecraft used the giant planet's *gravitational field* to pump up its energy and speed up, loop out of the orbital plane, and settle into an orbit that would take the spacecraft above the Sun's poles. *Ulysses* began its first pass over the Sun's south pole in the summer of 1994 and zoomed over the north pole in 1995. Then it began its second orbit of the mighty star. The little spacecraft's next close encounter with the Sun came in 2001.

At its most distant point from the Sun, the spacecraft is more than five times farther from the Sun than Earth is. Strangely, even its closest approach is farther from the Sun than Earth's orbit. Even though *Ulysses* is studying the Sun from a point in space that is always farther away from the Sun than Earth is, the spacecraft has provided a great deal of important information because it has a unique perspective. *Ulysses* carries a lot of equipment for onboard experiments to gain a better understanding of the *solar wind*, magnetic fields and particles, interplanetary dust and gas, the corona, and cosmic rays.

More Solar Spacecraft

Another capable observer was the *Yohkoh* solar probe. (*Yohkoh* means "sunbeam" in Japanese.) It was launched in 1991 by Japan, the United States, and the United Kingdom to study high-energy radiation from solar flares. The X-ray instrument on board helped scientists build a new understanding of the constant change and violence that take place within the Sun.

On December 2, 1995, NASA launched another joint ESA/NASA mission to the Sun. This one, the *Solar and Heliospheric Observatory (SOHO)*, set out to study the Sun's internal structure. It was launched into what is known as a "halo orbit," located about 1 million miles (1,528,500 km) from Earth and 92 million miles (150,703,500 km) from the Sun. *SOHO* is positioned at the point where Earth's gravitational pull is balanced by the Sun's gravity, giving astronomers a continuously clear view of the Sun. *SOHO's* powerful instruments monitor the Sun around the clock. They have provided "solar weather updates" and are currently studying the Sun's corona and inner layers.

In 1997 the United States placed the *Advanced Composition Explorer (ACE)* spacecraft in orbit to observe the solar wind, the Sun, and the galaxies beyond. It also orbits in halo orbit about 1 million miles (1,500,000 km) from Earth.

In 1999, another spacecraft, the *Transition Region and Coronal Explorer (TRACE)*, was launched by the United States for an extended mission to study the Sun's upper atmosphere. Like the many spacecraft that came before it, *TRACE* will help scientists gain a better understanding of our favorite star—the Sun.

The Conclusion is Open-Ended

The adventure of observing the universe has attracted some of the finest men and women in science. Over the centuries since ancient peoples first looked up at the skies and wondered, skywatchers have found many different ways to unlock the mysteries that beckon from such enormous distances. They thrive on the mysteries and puzzles, the vastness and variety of the objects found in galaxies and in the intergalactic regions, and the challenges of understanding the processes and makeup of everything surrounding us—always at vast distances. What are black holes? How do they interact with quasars? How did the universe form? How did everything that we see form and evolve? How can we find out more about them? What new techniques of observation can we use? Who will make the next great discovery about what makes the universe tick? Maybe, someday, it will be you.

A History of Observing: A Timeline

1608 — Dutch eyeglass maker Hans Lippershey builds the first refracting telescope.

1609 — Italian astronomer Galileo Galilei makes the first observations of celestial objects with a telescope he built.

1663 — Scottish mathematician James Gregory is first to think of using a mirror instead of a lens in a telescope.

1668 — Isaac Newton builds the first successful reflecting telescope.

1770s — William Herschel builds immense telescopes, as big as 48 inches (1.2 m) in diameter.

1844 — Lord Rosse builds an even bigger, 72-inch (1.8-m) telescope in Ireland.

1917 — The Hooker telescope, a reflector with a diameter of 100 inches (2.5 m) is completed at Mount Wilson Observatory, Pasadena, California.

1923	— Rocket scientist Hermann Oberth publishes a book about placing a telescope in orbit.
1946	— Astronomer Lyman Spitzer writes a report exploring in detail the idea of a telescope in orbit.
1948	— The Hale telescope obtains first light at the Palomar Mountain Observatory in California, at 200 inches (5 m) becoming the largest reflecting telescope in the world.
1957	— The USSR launches the first artificial satellite, *Sputnik 1.*
1972	— Launch of the first small astronomical telescope, *Copernicus,* the first of NASA's *Orbiting Astronomical Observatory* (*OAO*s).
1977	— Congress approves funding for a sophisticated space telescope, the first of NASA's Great Observatories, later named the *Hubble Space Telescope.*
1979	— NASA begins building the *Hubble.*

1990	*Hubble Space Telescope* is launched from the space shuttle *Discovery*.
	Flaw in primary mirror is discovered; approval and development of COSTAR (Corrective Optics Space Telescope Axial Replacement), a complex optical package to reduce distortion and slightly blurred images.
1991	The *Compton Gamma-Ray Observatory (CGRO)* is launched from the space shuttle *Atlantis*.
1993	The Keck I 386-inch (9.8 m) reflecting telescope is completed at the Mauna Kea Observatory in Hawaii, atop the 13,800-foot (4,200-m) summit of Mauna Kea.
1993	First servicing mission, space shuttle *Endeavour*. During EVAs, astronauts install COSTAR and perform other updates and repairs.
1996	Keck II is completed on Mauna Kea. With its twin (Keck I) it is the largest reflecting telescope in the world, using segmented reflecting mirrors.

1997	Second servicing mission to *HST*, space shuttle *Discovery*.
1999	*Chandra X-Ray Observatory*, another part of NASA's Great Observatories series, is launched and deployed from the space shuttle *Columbia*.
	Third servicing mission for *HST*, possibly extending its life for another 10 years.
2000	*Compton Gamma-Ray Observatory* completes its mission and is safely brought down from orbit.
2001	NASA's *2001 Mars Odyssey* arrives safely to orbit and studies the surface of Mars.
2002	Fourth servicing mission to *HST:* Improved camera, updated power source, and other instrument upgrades made.
2003	Three missions to Mars are launched in June: the UK's *Beagle 2*, ESA's *Mars Express,* and NASA's Mars Rover Spirit Mission.
	(planned) Launch of the Space Infrared Telescope Facility (SIRTF), the fouth member of NASA's Great Observatories Series.

2011 — (Planned) *James Webb Space Telescope* (*JWST*, or *"Hubble 2"*) formerly *Next Generation Space Telescope* (*NGST*), to be launched.

(Planned) Final servicing mission to bring *Hubble* mission to completion; plans exist to return Hubble to Earth so some instruments may be reused in other telescopes.

Glossary

asteroid—relatively large leftover chunks of material not included in any planet during formation; also, part of a planet broken off by a collision

asteroid belt—region between Mars and Jupiter, where most asteroids orbit

atmosphere—layer of gases surrounding an object in space, such as a planet or moon

aurora (pl. aurorae)—displays of light caused by interaction between energetic charged particles and a planet's magnetic field

black hole—an object in space having such extreme mass and density, and therefore extreme gravity, that it prevents all matter, as well as light, from escaping it, believed to have formed from a collapsed star.

CCD—abbreviation meaning "charge-coupled device," an instrument that uses a light-sensitive substance on a silicon chip to record images digitally, taking the place of a camera in many of today's telescopes.

composition—what something, such as a planet, is made of

comet—a small celestial body having a very elongated orbit around the Sun, with a head, or nucleus, composed of frozen water and gases mixed with dust; when nearing the Sun, the frozen material sublimates and forms a vast cloud of gas and grit and a tail of vapor.

concave—describing a lens or mirror, a shape that is thinner at the middle and thick at the edges, giving it a scooped-out appearance

convection cell—a heat-transfer cell, or region in a heated substance where heat is transferred by a circulation pattern created by heat differences

convex—describing a lens or mirror, a shape that is thicker at the middle and thin at the edges

core—the distinct region that is located at the center of a planet or moon; a body that has the same composition throughout is not said to have a core.

crater—a rimmed basin or depression in the surface of a planet or moon, caused by the impact of a meteorite

density—how much of a substance exists in a given volume; that is, the amount of mass in a given volume of a particular substance.

Each material has a specific density—so no matter how much you have, it always has the same density.

diameter—the distance across the center of a circle or sphere

electromagnetic spectrum—the full range of the waves and frequencies of electromagnetic radiation. Radio and infrared rays, at one end of the spectrum, have very long wavelengths and are invisible to human eyes. Visible light is about in the middle. At the other end of the spectrum are types of radiation with such short wavelengths that they are invisible to humans, including ultraviolet (UV) waves, X rays, and gamma rays.

gravitational field—the region around an object where its gravitational pull is felt

gravity—a force of attraction between two objects with mass, such as a star, planet, or moon; the attraction exerted by an object with mass. The gravity of the Moon creates the tides on Earth; Jupiter's gravity influences its moons and all nearby objects, including asteroids in the asteroid belt. Gravity keeps Earth orbiting the Sun and space observatories and space shuttles orbiting Earth.

interstellar—between or among the stars

light pollution—brightening of the nighttime sky that makes Earth-bound astronomy difficult; caused by artificial lights on Earth's surface

light year—the distance light travels through a vacuum in 1 year, about 5.88 trillion miles (9.46 trillion km)

magnetosphere—a vast region of electromagnetic radiation and electrically charged particles extending out from a planet; it is caused by the interaction of the planet's magnetic field and the solar wind.

mass—the amount of material a body contains; mass is measured in grams or kilograms; unlike weight, which varies with gravity, the mass of an object is the same wherever it is located.

meteorite—a chunk of a rock from space that has struck the surface of a planet or moon

nebula (pl. nebulae)—a cloud of interstellar gas or dust, or both; in the past, nebula has been used to refer to things we now know are galaxies

nuclear fusion—the process that takes place in the core of the Sun and other stars, releasing enormous energy when two atoms of a light element (hydrogen) combine to form one heavier atom (helium)

nucleus (pl. nuclei)—the head, or main body, of a comet

objective—the primary mirror or lens on a telescope; that is, the first lens or mirror struck by light shining into the telescope

optics—the optical devices (lenses and mirrors) that serve to relay light in a telescope

orbit—the path traced out by an object as it revolves around another body

quasar—(abbreviation for "quasi-stellar radio source"), a very bright, compact starlike object in space that is far away and moving rapidly away from us; the amount of radiation emitted by some quasars may greatly.

radio emissions—electromagnetic signals sent out in the frequency range between about 10 kilohertz and 300,000 megahertz; radio waves, like all other electromagnetic radiation, travel at the speed of light, 186,282 miles (300,000 km) per second in a vacuum.

reflector—a type of telescope that uses mirrors to gather light and relay images to the observer

refractor—a type of telescope that uses lenses to gather light and magnify objects *resolution*—in an image or photograph, the ability to display detail; a camera having high resolution can capture extensive detail with a high level of accuracy.

revolve—to move in a path, or orbit, around another object. The Earth revolves around the Sun, making a complete trip in one year.

rotate—to turn on its axis.

solar nebula—a primitive cloud of gas and material from which the Sun and the planets were born

solar wind—the rush of electrically charged particles emitted by the Sun, extending far out to the edge of the solar system; in fact, the "heliopause," or edge of the solar system, is defined as the point where the solar wind can no longer be detected.

telescope—an instrument used to view distant objects, especially useful for deep space

ultraviolet (UV) rays—radiation with wavelengths just shorter than violet light; "black light" is a form of UV radiation.

volume—the amount of space occupied by an object, expressed in three-dimensional terms such as cubic miles, cubic kilometers, and so on.

The news from space changes fast, so it's always a good idea to check the copyright date on books, CD-ROMs, and videotapes to make sure that you are getting up-to-date information. One good place to look for current information from NASA is U.S. government depository libraries. There are several in each state.

Books

Campbell, Ann Jeanette. *The New York Public Library Amazing Space: A Book of Answers for Kids.* New York: John Wiley & Sons, 1997.

Peterson, Carolyn Collins, and John C. Brandt. *Hubble Vision: Further Adventures with the Hubble Space Telescope.* Cambridge: Cambridge University Press, 1998.

Scott, Elaine, and Margaret Miller (photographer). *Adventure in Space: The Flight to Fix the Hubble.* New York: Hyperion Books for Children, 1995.

Spangenburg, Ray, and Kit Moser. *The Hubble Space Telescope.* Danbury, Conn.: Franklin Watts, 2002.

Sumners, Carolyn T., and Kerry Handron. *An Earthling's Guide to Deep Space. Explore the Galaxy Through the Eye of Hubble Space Telescope.* New York: McGraw-Hill, 1998.

Voit, Mark, and Richard Maurer. *Hubble Space Telescope: New Views of the Universe.* New York: Harry N. Abrams, 2000.

Videotapes

Hubble Telescope, Air & Space, 1997.
    VHS format

Hubble Space Telescope: Rescue in Space, 1995.
    VHS format

Organizations and Online Sites

These organizations and online sites are good sources of information about observing the universe, astronomy, and telescopes. Many of the online sites listed below are NASA sites, with links to many other interesting sources of information about the universe. You can also sign up to receive NASA news on many subjects via e-mail.

Amazing Space (Education Online from the Hubble Space Telescope)
http://amazing-space.stsci.edu
This site offers web-based activities, developed for students by the Space Telescope Science Institute. Activities cover topics from the history of telescopes to black holes and galaxies.

Astronomical Society of the Pacific
http://www.astrosociety.org
390 Ashton Avenue
San Francisco, CA 94112

Birr Castle

http://www.birrcastle.com

Celebrates the home and achievements of the great Irish telescope maker Lord Rosse.

Hubble: Cosmic Kids

http://sm3a.gsfc.nasa.gov/classrm.html

Great site for kids—uses cartoon characters to explore the *Hubble* and show how it works.

Hubble Site

http://sm3a.stsci.edu/

A wealth of information about Hubble provided as the Public Outreach site for the *Hubble Space Telescope.* It is produced by the Space Telescope Science Institute, which manages *Hubble* and the *Next Generation Space Telescope.*

Lunar and Planetary Institute

http://www.lpi.usra.edu/lpi.html

A NASA-funded institute that offers much fascinating material about space exploration and the solar system.

NASA: Ask a Space Scientist

http://image.gsfc.nasa.gov/poetry/ask/askmag.html#list

Take a look at the Interactive Page where NASA scientists answer your

questions about astronomy, space, and space missions. The site also has access to archives and fact sheets.

The Nine Planets: A Multimedia Tour of the Solar System
http://www.seds.org/nineplanets/nineplanets/nineplanets.html
This site has excellent material on the planets. It was created and is maintained by the Students for the Exploration and Development of Space, University of Arizona.

Planetary Missions
http://nssdc.gsfc.nasa.gov/planetary/projects.html
At this site, you'll find NASA links to all current and past missions. It's a one-stop shopping center to a wealth of information.

The Planetary Society
http://www.planetary.org/
65 North Catalina Avenue
Pasadena, CA 91106-2301

Real-Time Spacecraft Tracking
http://liftoff.msfc.nasa.gov/RealTime/JTrack/Spacecraft.html
Find out where the *Hubble Space Telescope* is orbiting right now, along with the *Chandra X-Ray Observatory*, the space shuttle (when in flight), the *International Space Station*, and other spacecraft.

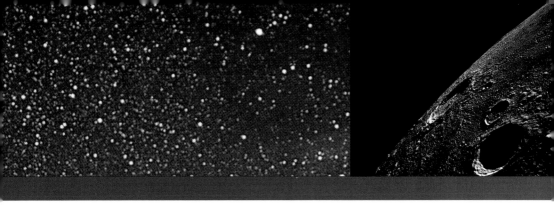

Space.Com

http://www.spacekids.com

A site just for kids about space, astronomy, cosmology, and planetary science—with clear explanations and an easy-to-read, upbeat approach.

Sky Online

http://www.skyandtelescope.com

This is the Web site for *Sky and Telescope* magazine and other publications of Sky Publishing Corporation. You'll find a good weekly news section on general space and astronomy news. The site also has tips for amateur astronomers as well as a nice selection of links. A list of science museums, planetariums, and astronomy clubs organized by state can help you locate nearby places to visit.

Welcome to the Planets

http://pds.jpl.nasa.gov/planets/

This tour of the solar system has lots of pictures and information. The site was created and is maintained by the California Institute of Technology for NASA/Jet Propulsion Laboratory.

Windows to the Universe

http://windows.ivv.nasa.gov/

This NASA site, developed by the University of Michigan, includes sections on "Our Planet," "Our Solar System," "Space Missions," and

"Kids' Space." Choose from presentation levels of beginner, intermediate, or advanced.

Places to Visit

Check the Internet (*www.skyandtelescope.com* is a good place to start), your local visitor's center, or phone directory for planetariums and science museums near you. Here are a few suggestions:

Ames Research Center
Moffett Field, CA 94035
http://www.arc.nasa.gov/
Located near Mountain View and Sunnyvale on the San Francisco Peninsula, Ames Research Center welcomes visitors. Drop-in visitors are welcome and admission is free.

Exploratorium
3601 Lyon Street
San Francisco, CA 94123
http://www.exploratorium.edu/
You'll find internationally acclaimed interactive science exhibits, including astronomy subjects.

National Air and Space Museum
7th and Independence Ave., S.W.
Washington, DC 20560
http://www.nasm.si.edu/
This Smithsonian museum, located on the National Mall west of the
Capitol building, has many interesting exhibits related to the history of
space exploration.

Rose Center for Earth and Space
American Museum of National History
New York, NY 10024
http://www.amnh.org/rose/
Exciting displays and presentations await in this premier planetarium
and space museum.

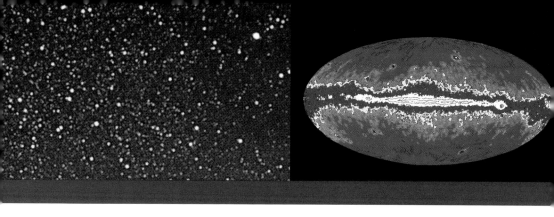

Ray Spangenburg and **Kit Moser** are a husband-and-wife writing team specializing in science and technology. They have written over 50 books and more than 100 articles, including a five-book series on the history of science and a four-book series on the history of space exploration. As journalists, they have covered NASA and related science activities for many years. They have flown on NASA's *Kuiper Airborne Observatory*, covered stories at the Deep Space Network in the Mojave Desert, and experienced zero gravity on experimental NASA flights out of NASA's Ames Research Center. They live in Carmichael, California, with their Boston terrier, F. Scott Fitz.

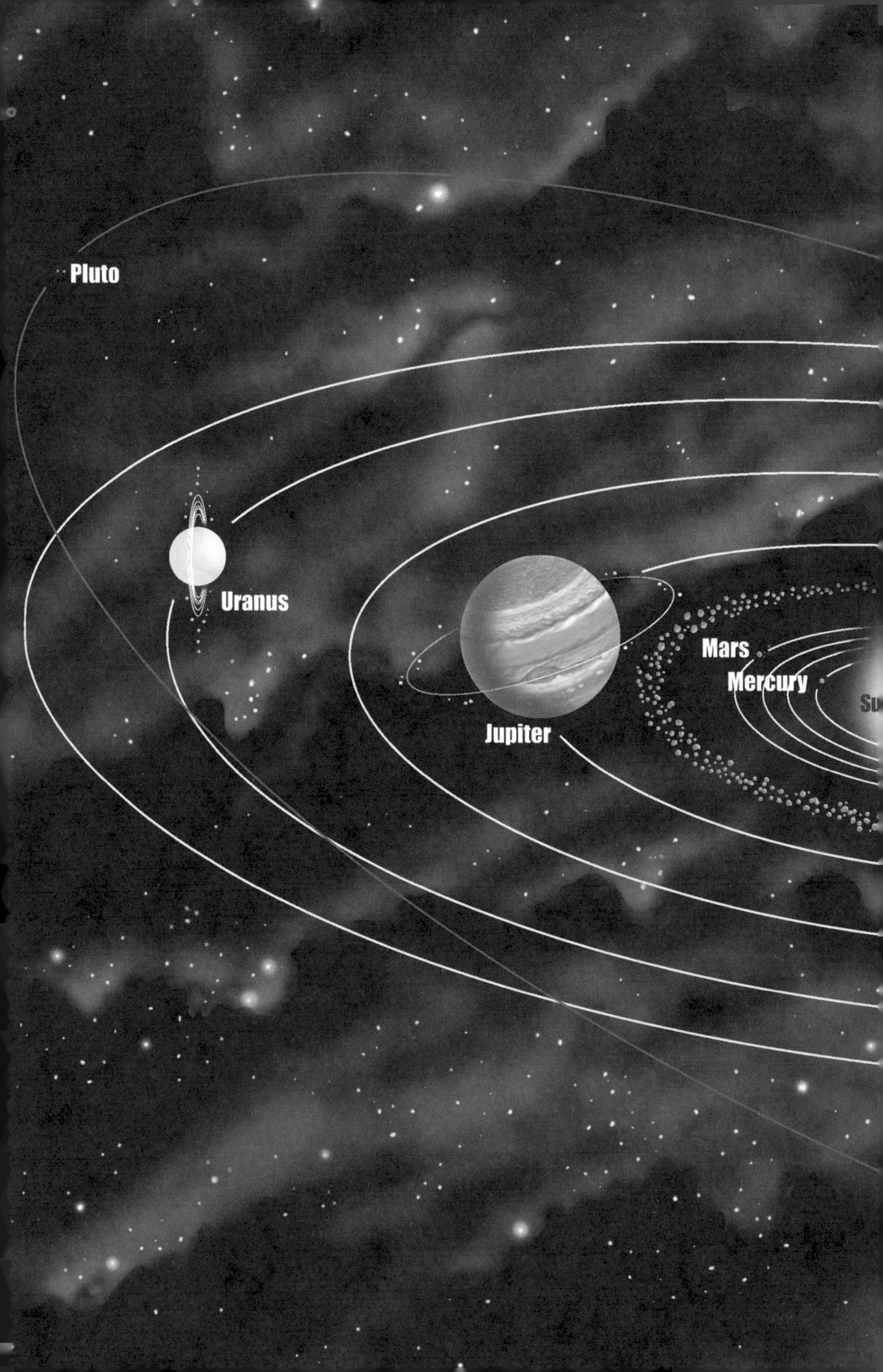

Pluto
Uranus
Jupiter
Mars
Mercury